OECD Public Governance Reviews

Integrity in the Peruvian Regions

IMPLEMENTING THE INTEGRITY SYSTEM

OECD

BETTER POLICIES FOR BETTER LIVES

This document, as well as any data and map included herein, are without prejudice to the status of or sovereignty over any territory, to the delimitation of international frontiers and boundaries and to the name of any territory, city or area.

Please cite this publication as:

OECD (2021), *Integrity in the Peruvian Regions: Implementing the Integrity System*, OECD Public Governance Reviews, OECD Publishing, Paris, *https://doi.org/10.1787/ceba1186-en*.

ISBN 978-92-64-47156-6 (print)
ISBN 978-92-64-39524-4 (pdf)

OECD Public Governance Reviews
ISSN 2219-0406 (print)
ISSN 2219-0414 (online)

Foreword

Integrity is a cornerstone of good governance, shaping democracies, economies and societies. It contributes to more efficient public sectors, more productive economies, more inclusive societies and greater public trust. The COVID-19 crisis accentuated the need for integrity to ensure that government action at all levels is effective and benefits those in need. The crisis unfortunately creates opportunities for integrity violations and could exacerbate fraud and corruption, particularly in public procurement, economic stimulus packages and social benefit programmes. Without a coherent integrity system in place that can identify and mitigate integrity vulnerabilities at both central and subnational levels, corruption can flourish during the crisis and undermine a country's social and economic recovery as well as its long-term resilience.

In Peru, the National Plan of Integrity and Fight against Corruption 2018-2021 (*Plan Nacional de Integridad y Lucha contra la Corrupción*) establishes a clear path towards creating a coherent integrity system. It underlines the crucial role of regional governments in mainstreaming integrity throughout the country. The Plan drew on the analysis and recommendations provided in the *OECD Integrity Review of Peru* of 2016, which put forward a strategic vision of integrity and actions to mainstream integrity throughout the whole of government and society. To achieve this goal, Peru mandated all public entities, including in regional governments, to establish an integrity function. While this is a significant step forward, ensuring their implementation is much more difficult, particularly at the regional and municipal level.

The report supports a better understanding of public integrity and its benefits for governments among regional political leaders. It guides the Secretariat of Public Integrity and other national actors in the implementation of the integrity function in the regions in a strategic and priority-based manner which builds commitment and ownership. Furthermore, the report underscores the Regional Anti-corruption Commissions as key actors that need to be strengthened to successfully control corruption in the Peruvian regions.

As such, the report builds on the *OECD Recommendation of the Council on Public Integrity* to establish clear responsibilities for integrity at all levels of government. Indeed, the breadth of responsibilities, planning and licensing discretions, and close proximity to citizens and users of government services place subnational governments at a unique conjunction of integrity challenges. It is often at this level where trust is forged or lost, given the close interaction between government, the private sector and citizens. At the same time, formal accountability measures are at times weaker than at the national level.

The establishment of integrity functions in the regional governments and enabling the Regional Anti-corruption Commission to fulfil their mandate will contribute towards incorporating integrity in public management and effectively strengthen an integrity culture throughout the country. It is a clear step towards preventing corruption and fraud, strengthening citizens' trust and contributing to inclusive growth in Peru.

Acknowledgements

The report was prepared by the OECD Public Sector Integrity Division of the Directorate of Public Governance under the leadership of Julio Bacio Terracino. The report was co-ordinated and guided by Frédéric Boehm and drafted by Giulio Nessi and Felicitas Neuhaus. Maria Varinia Michalun of the OECD Centre for Entrepreneurship, SMEs, Regions and Cities provided key comments and inputs. Meral Gedik, Balazs Gyimesi and Andrea Uhrhammer supported the team in editing, designing the layout and producing the report. Aleksandra Bogusz, Rania Haidar and Charles Victor provided administrative assistance. The Spanish translation of the Review was prepared by Carmen Navarrete and edited by Rosana Vargas.

We thank the financial and technical support given by the German Development Cooperation, implemented by Deutsche Gesellschaft für Internationale Zusammenarbeit (GIZ) GmbH, in particular the support of the "Anti-corruption and Integrity Programme" and the comments made by the Project team in Peru of the "Citizen-oriented state reform Programme (Good Governance)" led by Mayra Ugarte and supported by Florian Schatz. The OECD also thanks the former head of the GIZ good governance programme in Peru, Hartmut Paulsen, for his guidance and support.

The OECD expresses its gratitude to the Peruvian Government, in particular, the Secretariat of Public Integrity of the Presidency of the Council of Ministers (SIP), led by Eloy Munive Pariona, Secretary of Public Integrity, and his team. The former Secretary of Public Integrity, Susana Silva Hasembank, as well as Cristina Arvildo, Fernando Hurtado and Vladimir Léon from the SIP significantly supported and co-ordinated the project activities, including the fact-finding mission carried out in November 2019, and provided guidance and feedback throughout the project. The OECD would also like to thank the institutions and organisations who took part in the process and provided valuable information for the elaboration of the report, in particular the regional governments and regional control offices as well as the members of the Regional Anti-Corruption Commissions of Cajamarca, Lambayeque, and San Martin; the National Civil Service Authority (*Autoridad Nacional del Servicio Civil*, SERVIR); the Secretariat for Decentralisation (*Secretaría de Descentralización*); the Public Administration Secretariat (*Secretaría de Gestión Pública*, or SGP); the Office of the Comptroller General (*Contraloría General de la República*, or CGR) and the Ombudsman Office (*Defensoría del Pueblo*). The preliminary version of the report was presented and discussed during a virtual event with the SIP and representatives of the integrity function from regional governments on 17 September 2020 as well as during a virtual meeting of the international co-operation community in Peru on 2 October 2020. The report also benefitted from the invaluable insights and comments of Limberg Chero, Juan Carlos Cortés Carcelén, Fiorella Mayaute, Mirtha Muñiz, Carlos Vargas, and Eduardo Vega.

The review was approved by the OECD Working Party of Senior Public Integrity Officials (SPIO) on 3 December 2020 and declassified by the Public Governance Committee on 28 December 2020.

Table of contents

FIGURES

TABLES

Follow OECD Publications on:

http://twitter.com/OECD_Pubs

http://www.facebook.com/OECDPublications

http://www.linkedin.com/groups/OECD-Publications-4645871

http://www.youtube.com/oecdilibrary

http://www.oecd.org/oecddirect/

Abbreviations and acronyms

AMPE	Association of Municipalities of Peru
ANGR	National Assembly of Regional Governments
CAN	High-level Commission against Corruption
CAS	Administrative Service Contract
CEPLAN	Centre for National Strategic Planning
CGR	Office of the Comptroller General of the Republic
CRA	Regional Anti-corruption Commission
ENAP	National Public Administration School
ESAP	National School of Public Administration (Colombia)
EVA	Virtual Advisory Space (Colombia)
FP	Administrative Department of Public Service (Colombia)
GORE	Regional Governments
GIZ	German International Co-operation (*Deutsche Gesellschaft für Internationale Zusammenarbeit*)
HR	Human Resources
INEI	National Institute of Statistics
MEF	Ministry of Economy and Finance
MP	Attorney General Office
OCI	Offices of Institutional Control
OECD	Organisation for Economic Co-operation and Development
OII	Offices of Institutional Integrity
OSCE	Government Procurement Supervising Agency
PC	Central Purchasing Body
PCM	Presidency of the Council of Ministers
PNILC	National Policy of Integrity and Fight Against Corruption 2018-2021
RDA	Regional Development Agency
REMURPE	Network of Urban and Rural Municipalities of Peru
ROF	Organisational and Functions Regulation

SERVIR	National Civil Service Authority
SGP	Secretariat of Public Management
SIP	Secretariat of Public Integrity
SWOT	Strengths, Weaknesses, Opportunities, and Threats
TI	Transparency International

Executive summary

Regional integrity systems in Peru depend on a number of policies, actors and mechanisms operating at the central, regional and municipal levels. While Peru has put in place a strategy and a formal co-ordination framework, regional governments remain highly affected by corruption. The level of policy implementation and institutional activity on public integrity is generally limited and not able to generate significant impact.

A combination of national and regional factors determine corruption in regional governments

The Peruvian National Integrity and Anti-corruption Policy recognises that subnational entities are those most affected by corruption while anti-corruption actions at these levels are often limited. In consequence, the Action Plan for 2018-2021 defines several actions for regional governments, including the establishment of an integrity function in charge of the articulation and monitoring of the integrity framework to be implemented in each entity (the "integrity model").

However, the implementation of the integrity function and model in regional governments is lagging behind that of central government entities. So far, only five regions have appointed a unit or person in charge of the integrity function. Reasons for this are manifold and due to a number of contextual and resources-related factors, including high regional diversity, enduring challenges in completing the decentralisation process, the governors' limited awareness of the relevance and the benefits of integrity policies, regional politics, budget constraints, and a high degree of staff turnover.

An incremental approach based on priorities, capacity and integrity risks could promote an effective implementation of the regional integrity function

While the current legal framework already provides for a range of options for institutionalising the integrity function, the reality at regional level requires a more tailored and incremental approach based on available capacities and main integrity risks. The Secretariat of Public Integrity (SIP) could develop a matrix based on those dimensions, assigning each region to a category with a recommended institutional set-up and a list of functions to be prioritised. Such an approach would allow a gradual implementation of the full integrity function, focusing on articulating integrity policies and providing strategic orientation to leadership, especially to the Governor. Minimum tasks that should be ensured in all regional governments include identifying integrity risks, proposing concrete integrity policies and monitoring the integrity model's implementation.

In addition, each regional government should define a number of priority areas where integrity policies should be applied. This could be done through an assessment of the internal strengths and weaknesses and external opportunities and threats of the regional government. Priority areas could include, for instance, the safeguarding of the achievement of policy goals related to SDGs, mining, health, education or infrastructure.

The integrity function increases the impact of the Regional Anticorruption Commissions

Following the model of the National Anticorruption Commission (CAN), the Regional Anticorruption Commissions (CRAs) involve various stakeholders from public and private sectors. While this design seeks to co-ordinate efforts at regional level, experience so far shows that the CRAs have only a limited impact. Their impact is often undermined by political dynamics, conflicts among the members and failure to ensure relevant technical input, institutionalise the work or focus on strategic prevention and priorities.

To address these challenges, the CRAs could involve additional regional actors overseeing key processes and risks (such as in public procurement), standardise internal rules of procedure and ensure continuous engagement, in particular by appointing technical contact points within all member organisations. Most crucially, the integrity function could be designated as the technical secretariat of the CRAs in order to leverage its integrity mandate in regional governments, avoid duplication of efforts, and ensure coherence with the National Policy. Furthermore, it could serve as the link between the regional government, the CRA, the CAN and the SIP to report on progress and good practices, but also to request technical assistance and political support.

National actors can also support regional integrity

In line with Peru's decentralised institutional model, a number of national actors have direct and indirect influence on regional governments' integrity systems and policies, and can thus provide support to the integrity function and system at the regional level.

Considering the limited capacities and resources at regional level, the SIP could scale up existing assistance to regional governments. In particular, it could mobilise high-level commitment by illustrating and clarifying public integrity concepts and pointing out the economic benefits, especially in the current COVID-19 emergency context. The SIP could also build the capacities of staff working in the regions' integrity function and promote dialogue between the integrity functions. Currently, such an exchange only takes place on an informal and occasional basis.

In turn, the CAN could provide strategic direction to strengthen the technical secretariats of the CRAs through a capacity development strategy and a mechanism to ensure the sharing of information and experience among regions to improve mutual learning around risks, achievements and priority issues. The CAN could also host a platform to monitor and benchmark public integrity in the regions through indicators that measure, for instance, the implementation and the performance of the integrity functions and of the CRAs. Since societal actors in the regions often are unaware of integrity efforts and initiatives, the CAN could support the CRAs by promoting online training courses on public integrity policies and their benefits in close collaboration with universities and civil society at the regional level.

Finally, the Presidency of the Council of Ministers could also promote co-ordination efforts and provide concrete support to regional integrity systems. In particular, the establishment of Regional Development Agencies (RDA) is a major opportunity to advance the decentralisation process but also entails various integrity risks. As such, the regional integrity function could provide RDA with advice on identifying and mitigating these integrity risks, in particular those related to undue influence in decision-making processes or conflict of interest.

1 Introduction

This Chapter provides an introduction to the report. It highlights Peru's key political and geographical characteristics and calls for the need to strengthen the integrity policies of the Regional Governments, aiming at building coherent integrity sub-systems aligned with the national integrity system.

Peru is a unitary state, about twice the size of France in land-mass, with a two-tier subnational system of government composed of 24 regions and the constitutional province of Callao, 1 874 district municipalities and 196 provincial municipalities. The provincial municipalities have a co-ordination role across district municipalities. Overall, Peru has a complex system of shared and exclusive competences between the three levels of government (national, regional and municipal).

The territory can be broadly divided into three zones, the coast (*costa*), the uplands (*sierra*) and the rainforest (*selva*) and each zone has certain geographic and socio-demographic commonalities. Nonetheless, the 24 regions and the constitutional province all have different levels of development and face different integrity challenges. Expanding a framework for high-quality regulation at all levels of government is a challenge for all countries and can only be achieved if countries take into consideration the diversity of subnational needs and the particularities of lower levels of government (Rodrigo, Allio and Andres-Amo, 2009[1]).

This also applies to the implementation of a public integrity system at all levels of government as encouraged by the *OECD Recommendation of the Council on Public Integrity* (OECD, 2017[2]). In fact and as will be analysed in detail in the sub-section on "Regional and other subnational governments are highly vulnerable to corruption" in Chapter 2, subnational entities in Peru experience specific integrity challenges and high risks of corruption, just like in other countries in Latin America and worldwide (OECD, 2019[3]; OECD, 2018[4]). For example, according to the Anticorruption Prosecution Office (*Procuraduría Pública Especializada en Delitos de Corrupción*), 67 governors and former governors were under investigation in 2017 for corruption offences (Procuraduría Pública Especializada en Delitos de Corrupción, 2017[5]).

This situation underscores the need for Peru´s regional governments to strengthen their integrity efforts and build coherent integrity sub-systems aligned with the national integrity system. While formally a comprehensive framework for regional public integrity sub-systems is in place, in practice the level of policy implementation and institutional activity varies from region to region and depends on several contextual and resources-related factors, such as the prevailing integrity vulnerabilities, the availability of financial and human resources and their capacities, the political commitment and similar. The Peruvian National Integrity and Anticorruption Policy (*Política Nacional de Integridad y Lucha contra la Corrupción, PNILC*) recognises the limited reach of anti-corruption actions at the regional and local level, also in light of the evidence that subnational entities are those most affected by corruption.

Building on the previous integrity work of the OECD with Peru, this report focuses on the regional reality, assessing key challenges hindering the implementation of integrity systems at the regional level in the Peruvian context. It further proposes an incremental and realistic approach towards the implementation of the integrity function by regional governments. Furthermore, the report addresses how such an integrity function could support the regional anti-corruption co-ordination mechanism established in each region, the Regional Anti-corruption Commissions (*Comisiones Regionales Anticorrupción*, CRAs), which so far have demonstrated only a limited progress and impact. The regional focus of the report is not meant to underestimate other key challenges, actors and perspectives at the subnational level such as those in municipalities, but it is meant to address integrity risks and potential strategy within the weakest link in Peru's system of government (OECD, 2016[6]). Although in the last twenty years Peru has made strong advances in terms of political decentralisation, the process has not been fully completed and the regional level is highly affected by gaps and shortcomings.

Although the analysis of the report is strongly rooted in the regional challenges and context, the point of view taken to elaborate the recommendations is the national one, since the national integrity policy and related integrity obligations are to be implemented equally in regions, guided by the Public Integrity Secretariat (*Secretaría de Integridad Pública*, SIP). Furthermore, national actors still have a strong influence on regional policies and politics and should promote an enabling environment for integrity. From this perspective, the SIP has the key role of articulating both the horizontal co-ordination among national entities and the implementation of the national integrity system at the regional level.

References

OECD (2019), *La Integridad Pública en América Latina y el Caribe 2018-2019: De Gobiernos reactivos a Estados proactivos*, OECD, Paris, http://www.oecd.org/gov/integridad/integridad-publica-en-america-latina-caribe-2018-2019.htm (accessed on 25 February 2020).   [3]

OECD (2018), *Integrity for Good Governance in Latin America and the Caribbean: From Commitments to Action*, OECD Publishing, Paris, https://dx.doi.org/10.1787/9789264201866-en.   [4]

OECD (2017), *OECD Recommendation of the Council on Public Integrity*, OECD/LEGAL/0435, https://legalinstruments.oecd.org/en/instruments/OECD-LEGAL-0435.   [2]

OECD (2016), *OECD Territorial Reviews: Peru 2016*, OECD Territorial Reviews, OECD Publishing, Paris, https://dx.doi.org/10.1787/9789264262904-en.   [6]

Procuraduría Pública Especializada en Delitos de Corrupción (2017), *Sospecha generalizada de corrupción contra gobernadores y alcaldes del país*, https://plataformaanticorrupcion.pe/wp-content/uploads/2017/07/INFORME-CORRUPCION-SOBRE-GOBERNADORES-Y-ALCALDES.pdf (accessed on 6 November 2020).   [5]

Rodrigo, D., L. Allio and P. Andres-Amo (2009), "Multi-Level Regulatory Governance: Policies, Institutions and Tools for Regulatory Quality and Policy Coherence", *OECD Working Papers on Public Governance*, No. 13, OECD Publishing, Paris, https://dx.doi.org/10.1787/224074617147.   [1]

2 Strengthening integrity in the Peruvian regions

While integrity is a concern at all levels of government, opportunities for certain types of corruption risks can be more pronounced at subnational levels. In turn, strengthening integrity contributes to maximise the potential of subnationational entities in business activity, revenue collection and private and public investments. In Peru, a comprehensive framework exists for regional public integrity systems. In practice, however, the level of implementation varies from region to region and depends on several national but also contextual and resource-related factors.

Regional and other subnational governments are highly vulnerable to corruption

Subnational governments (states, provinces, municipalities, etc.) can be drivers for innovation, economic development and productivity and also play a key role in promoting social capital and well-being. However, weak governance structures can undermine their ability to do so. Vulnerabilities in governance structures and processes due to lack of integrity, transparency and accountability provide opportunities for corrupt practices and policy capture. At the same time, those benefitting from corruption have incentives to maintain the status quo and undermine effective reforms. In this way, corruption perpetuates and exacerbates governance weaknesses. A lack of integrity undermines the institutional capacity of the subnational government to effectively deliver public services and hinders the design and implementation of effective public policies. At the same time, when citizens do not perceive their government to be working in the public interest and deliver public service effectively, public trust can be undermined (OECD, 2018[1]).

In turn, strengthening integrity can mitigate the risk of corruption and policy capture, thereby contributing to the maximisation of a subnational area's full potential in business activity, revenue collection, and foreign and domestic private and public investments. Similarly, the subnational level may set an example for (re-)building trust and fighting threats, such as organised crime (OECD, 2018[1]).

While integrity is a concern at all levels of government, opportunities for certain types of corruption can be more pronounced at subnational levels. The increased frequency and closeness of interactions between subnational government authorities with citizens and firms as compared to the national level can create both opportunities, especially by facilitating subnational accountability, and risks for integrity. Subnational government responsibilities for the delivery of a large share of public services (e.g. education, health, security/justice, waste management, utilities, granting licences and permits) as well as for spending and investment, increase the frequency and directness of interactions between government authorities and citizens and firms, which creates opportunities to test the integrity of subnational governments (OECD, 2017[2]). Regional and local governments may also have higher levels of at-risk expenditure such as social spending or public procurement contracts, which require additional measures of control. For example, in 2015, 63% of public procurement spending occurred at the subnational level in the OECD (OECD, 2017[3]).

In general, OECD experience identifies a series of common challenges that may lead to opportunities for corruption at the subnational level, including in Peru's regional governments. These challenges are related to:

- Limited technical and financial capacities and resources.
- Higher discretion of subnational politicians due to often limited opposition, limited independence and effectiveness of subnational auditors, limited disclosure requirements for annual budget, public tenders and similar.
- Low capacities to issue and/or enforce regulations of good quality with direct impact on business activity and life of citizens.
- Insufficient safeguards for the independence of subnational enforcement systems, and lack of resources and capacity to effectively combat corruption.
- Close ties between business elites and political elites at the subnational level, leading to clientelistic practices.
- Weak presence of the State in remote rural areas.
- Weakness of subnational election processes, practices of vote-buying and patronage undermining the integrity of the electoral process.
- Limited ability by organised civil society (low capacities, capture of civil society groups, etc.) holding subnational governments to account for their actions.
- Unclear assignment of responsibilities across levels of governments limiting co-ordination and accountability.

- Mismatch between responsibilities and financial resources of subnational governments. The limited fiscal autonomy might undermine subnational accountability.
- Governance arrangements to co-ordinate priorities and align objectives are often weak. This directly affects the efficiency of public investments and spending.
- Poor data collection and performance monitoring of public service delivery and investments affect the needs assessment and the monitoring and evaluation of measures (OECD, 2018[1]).

In Peru, the anti-corruption efforts made by regional governments are perceived by the citizens as rather ineffective: 60% of Peruvians consider the efforts of the regional government as bad or very bad compared to 28% for the national government (Figure 2.1) (Proética, 2019[4]). This may be explained by a number of corruption cases involving the regional political leadership: in 2017, 67 of governors and former governors were under investigation for corruption offences. (Procuraduría Pública Especializada en Delitos de Corrupción, 2017[5]) This underscores the need for the regional governments to strengthen their integrity efforts and build a coherent integrity system aligned to the overall integrity system promoted at the central level.

Figure 2.1. Perception of the effectiveness of anti-corruption efforts made by Regional and National Governments

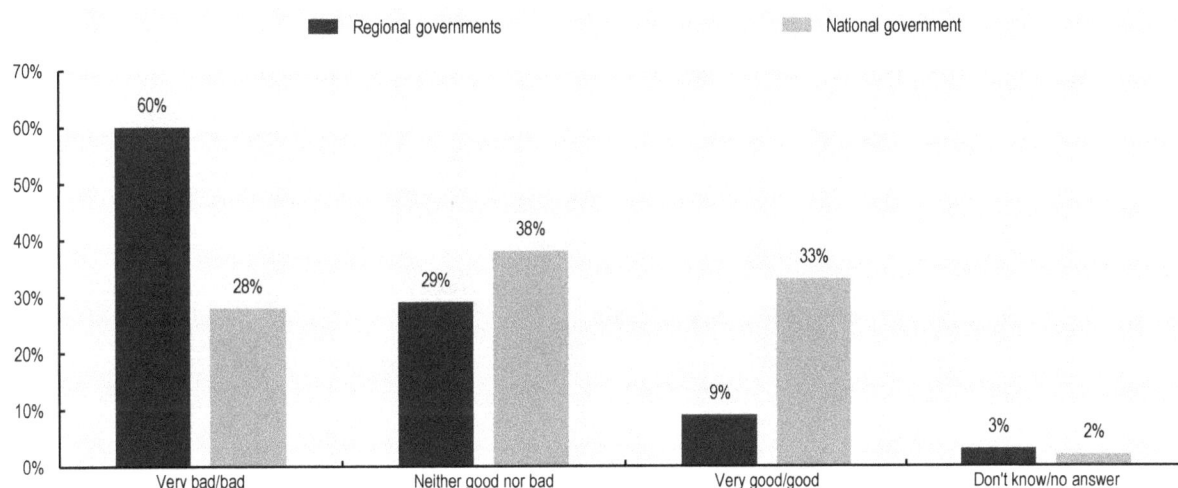

Note: Question posed to the respondents to the survey was: "According to your knowledge, how would you qualify the way the National Regional Government/Government in power manages the fight against corruption?" (*Según lo que usted conoce, ¿cómo calificaría la gestión de Gobiernos Regionales/Gobierno de turno en la lucha contra la corrupción?*).
Source: (Proética, 2019[4]).

The integrity ecosystem in Peru's regions

The current integrity ecosystem at regional level consists of and is determined by a number of policies, actors and mechanisms operating at both the central and regional level. While overall they formally compose a comprehensive framework for regional public integrity systems, in practice the level of policy implementation and institutional activity varies from region to region and depends on several contextual and resource-related factors.

The National Integrity and Anti-corruption Policy and its Action Plan 2018-2021

The National Integrity and Anti-corruption Policy, adopted with Decree N° 092-2017-PCM, provides for a comprehensive diagnostic of corruption and its causes in Peru and defines three themes of priority actions: preventive capacity, risk identification and management, and enforcing capacity. Each of these themes consists of specific objectives with related responsibilities and guidelines. Furthermore, the policy defines a number of minimum standards on various issues such as culture of integrity, conflict of interest, and electoral systems. This policy also built on the input of the *OECD Integrity Review of Peru* (OECD, 2017[6]) and a consultative commission of experts created by the President of Peru in 2016 (*Comisión Presidencial de Integridad)* which identified key risks and proposed a set of measures to promote integrity in the public sector (Comisión Presidencial de Integridad, 2017[7]).

The national policy recognises the limited reach of anti-corruption actions at the regional and local level, also in light of the evidence that subnational entities are those most affected by corruption. According to the criminal statistics of corruption cases reported in the national policy itself, cases in district municipalities accounted for 27.3% of the total (8 994 cases), followed by those in Municipal Provincial entities with 15.1% (4 985 cases), and Regional Governments with 10.2% (3 349 cases). Altogether they represented 52.6% of total cases at the national level, with a total amount of 17 328 cases. The increasing number of corruption cases at the subnational level are also pointed out in a report from Peru's Ombudsman Office comparing the criminal proceedings on corruption-related offences by public officials in 2016 and 2018 (Figure 2.2).

Figure 2.2. Criminal proceedings against public officials on corruption by department in 2016 and 2018

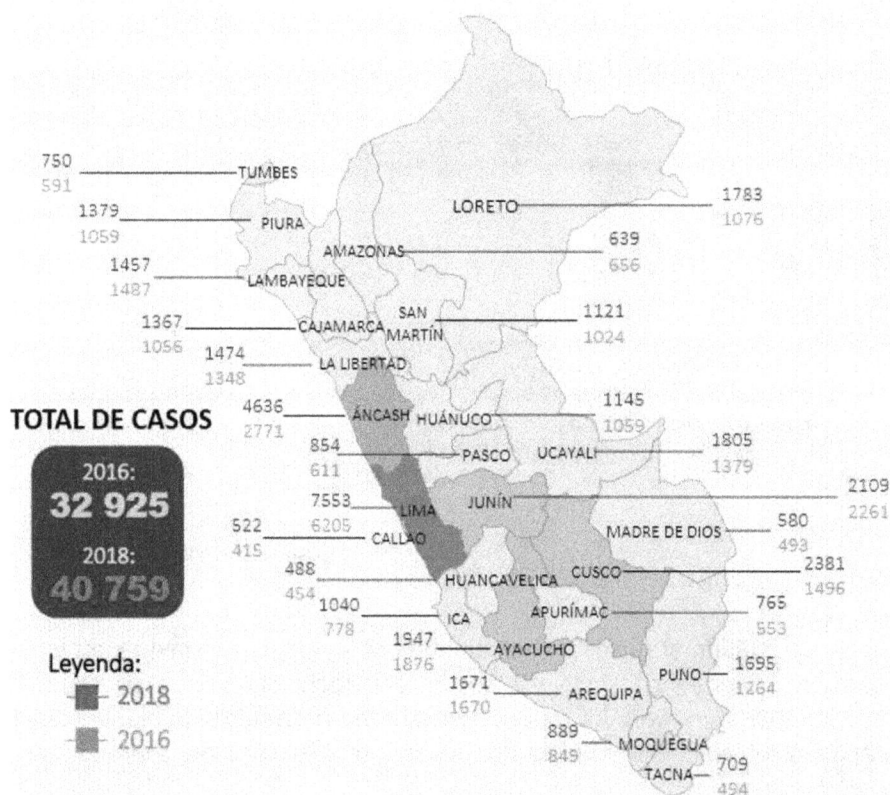

Note: The data correspond to the alleged crimes by public officials under the scope of Articles 326 and 401 of the Criminal Code.
Source: (Defensoría del Pueblo, 2019[8]).

The National Integrity and Anti-corruption Policy is complemented by an Action Plan for 2018-2021 (*Plan Nacional de Integridad y Lucha contra la Corrupción 2018-2021*) through Decree N° 044-2018-PCM, which defines several actions with specific goals (*metas*) involving regional governments. These are:

- Strengthening the Anti-corruption Commission (CAN) through the articulation of the Regional Anti-corruption Commissions (CRAs).
- Methodology for risk identification and management to prevent, detect and sanction corruption.
- Induction training for public officials.
- Performance management.
- Awareness-raising activities.
- Registration of lobbying activities (*registro de visitas*).
- Risk identification and management in public procurement processes, including training.
- Incorporation of institutional control bodies (*Oficinas de Control Institucional*, OCI) into the administrative structure of the Comptroller General Office (CGR).
- Administrative simplification.
- Compliance with transparency obligations.
- Accountability hearings and promotion of civil society training.
- Citizens oversight mechanisms.
- Digital technologies for accountability.
- School education on integrity.

More generally, both the anti-corruption policy and plan establish that the CRAs collaborate and support the SIP in the follow up, monitoring and evaluation of the plan itself.

Regional Anti-corruption Commissions

As emerging from both the National Policy and its Action Plan, the CRAs play a crucial role in co-ordinating the integrity and anti-corruption efforts in the regions. They are first envisaged in Law 29976 creating the National Anticorruption Commission and its implementing regulation (Decree N° 089-2013-PCM) as the entities co-responsible for implementing the National Policy with the CAN. For this creation, the legal framework indicates to take into account the structure, functions and participants of the CAN, in view of the adequate involvement of the key public actors, the business sector and civil society involved in the fight against corruption at the regional level. To further ensure co-ordination with the regional level, the CAN itself also counts with the participation, as full member, of the President of the National Assembly of Regional Governments.

In 2016, the Technical Secretariat of the CAN provided guidance for the creation of the CRAs, including on:

- the formal constitution through regional ordinance (*ordenanza regional*)
- the suggested composition, in line with the one of the CAN (Table 2.1)
- priority functions, which are:
  - the development of regional anti-corruption plans based on a corruption risk diagnosis (Box 2.1)
  - the follow-up, supervision, and reporting of the National Plan's compliance
  - proposing regional policies for the prevention and fight against corruption.
- the structure, with a rotating 1-year presidency among members and a technical secretariat to steer the technical work of the CAN

- the CRAs' internal regulation (*reglamento interno*), which should address the aim and objectives, the members' obligations and powers, functions of the President and the Technical Secretariat, as well as details on the organisation and development of the sessions (CAN, 2016[9]).

The CAN envisages a 60-day deadline for the adoption of the internal regulation starting at the first session of the CRA. In practice, it can be observed that not all active CRAs comply with this deadline and have adopted an internal regulation (21 out of 23 CRAs) (Table 2.2). Regarding the nomination of a Technical Secretary, 19 out of 23 active CRAs have so far done so. Furthermore, the institutions nominated for the role of the Presidency and the Technical Secretariat of the CRAs are playing a key role in the planning of activities and the provision of technical inputs. Currently the former is mostly given to the President of the High Court of Justice (Figure 2.3), while the latter to the Regional Government itself (Figure 2.4).

Box 2.1. CAN's Guidance on developing Regional Anticorruption Plans

The CAN stresses that the development of the Regional Anti-Corruption Plan is a priority area to be developed by the Regional Anti-Corruption Commission. It represents a management instrument allowing to focus on preventive and punitive actions based on the identification and assessment of the processes and practices that generate the greatest risk or vulnerability to corruption in each region. For this purpose, the CAN emphasises the preparation of a preparatory internal diagnosis in the region that should involve the participation of all relevant entities in the region. Guidance is also provided in identifying relevant actors in the preventive area, including those in charge of improving management, efficiency transparency, and oversight.

Source: (CAN, 2016[9]).

Table 2.1. Members of the CRAs

National institution	CRA's member	Role and function of the regional entity
Judicial Power (*Poder Judicial*)	President of the High Court of Justice (*Corte Superior de Justicia*)	The High Court of Justice is the highest judicial body in each judicial district.
Presidency of the Council of Ministers	Regional Governor	The mission of regional governments is to organise and lead the regional public management in line with the regions' exclusive, shared and delegated responsibilities, and within the framework of the national and sectoral policies. This should contribute to the region's integral and sustainable development. (Regional Governments Organic Law N° 27867)
Ministry of Justice and Human Rights	Decentralised Anti-corruption Public Prosecutor (*Procurador Público Descentralizado*)	The Anticorruption Attorney Office exercises the defence of the State to safeguard its interests through the collection of civil reparations and recovery of assets in cases of corruption involving public officials. The Office counts with 15 Decentralised Offices with responsibility on groups of judicial districts as defined by Resolution 046-2015-JUS/CDJE
Office of the Attorney General (*Fiscalía de la Nación*)	President of the Judicial Districts' Senior Prosecutors Council (*Junta de Fiscales Superiores del Distrito Judicial*)	Each Judicial District where are three or more Senior Prosecutors constitutes a Council, where prosecution activities are planned and organised under the supervision of its President. (Organic Law of the Public Prosecution Office, Legislative Decree N°052)
President of the National Assembly of Regional Governments (*Asamblea Nacional de Gobiernos Regionales*)	President/Representative of the Regional Council	Regional Councils are the democratically elected organs at regional level with regulatory function and supervising the Regional Government. Each Council counts with a President, a Vice-president, and 7 to 25 Councillors for each province that are elected for a 4 year-term.

National institution	CRA's member	Role and function of the regional entity
Office of the Comptroller General (*Contraloría General dela República*)	Head of the Regional Control Office (*Oficina Regional de Control*)	The Regional Control Offices are decentralised bodies of the Comptroller General Office with the responsibility to plan, organise, manage, execute and evaluate control activities in the entities under their jurisdiction.
Ombudsman Office (*Defensoría del Pueblo*)	Head of the Regional Ombudsman Office	The Ombudsman office has the institutional responsibility to defend and promote the rights of individuals, monitor the effectiveness of the State performance's administration and oversee the adequate provision of public services. At the regional level, it counts with 28 regional offices (Regional Governments Organic Law N° 27867).

Source: (CAN, 2016[9]).

Table 2.2. The implementation status of CRAs in Peru

	Status
Active CRAs in Regions[1]	92% (23 out of 25 Regional Governments)
CRAs with Technical Secretariat	83% (19 out of 23 CRAs)
CRAs' Technical Secretariat with full time dedicated Technical Secretary	0%
CRAs adopting Internal Regulation	91% (21 out of 23 CRAs)
CRAs adopting Regional AC Plan	56% (13 out of 23 CRAs)

1. A CRA is considered active when meets regularly, implements actions agreed upon in the Regional Plan or is in the process of elaborating it.
Source: Peru's Secretariat of Public Integrity, information as of January 2020; (Defensoria del Pueblo, 2018[10]).

Figure 2.3. Presidency of the CRAs

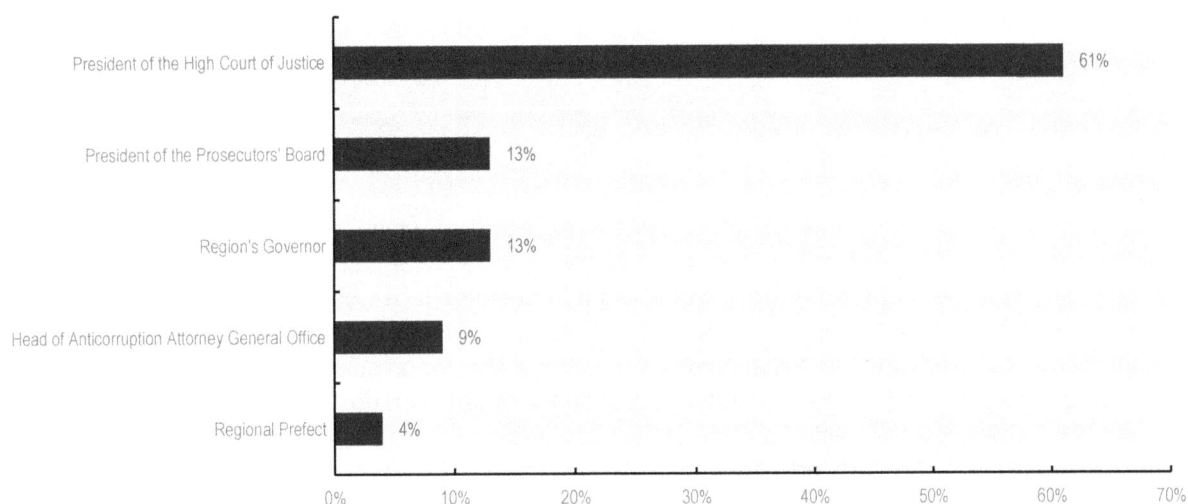

Source: SIP, January 2020.

Figure 2.4. Technical Secretariats of the CRAs

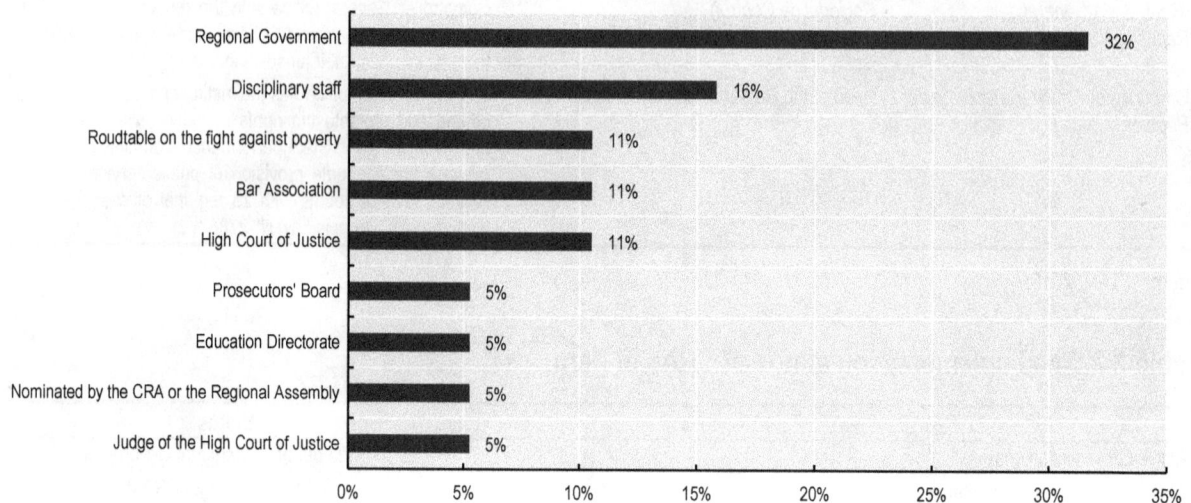

Note: Of a total of 19 Technical Secretariats.
Source: SIP, January 2020.

Furthermore, detailed indications with timelines have been developed by the CAN to assist the CRAs in the preparation of regional anti-corruption plans. The CAN estimates a total of 14 weeks for all the activities leading up to the plan. Accordingly, these should be developed addressing in sequence the following steps:

Figure 2.5. Steps for the development of Regional Anticorruption Plans

Source: (CAN, 2015[11]).

In this process, particular emphasis is made on the assessment which should aim at identifying the problems and conditions that facilitate corruption at the regional level, especially in relation to existing prevention and enforcement mechanisms, but also understanding those connected to the procurement processes and those of the key productive activities of each region. The guidance document on the plan also includes a proposed structure touching on all the above-mentioned steps of the process. In practice, however, it can be observed that Regional Anticorruption Plans are often not in place - this is the case only in 13 out of 23 active CRAs (Table 2.2). Those that are in place, are often not developed in a strategic manner. In many cases, they are not based on an assessment of integrity vulnerabilities and neglect the design of outcomes and indicators to facilitate monitoring and evaluation. They often consist of a tick-the-box exercise.

The implementation of the integrity model and function in the regions

The Peruvian Integrity Model

A key element of the integrity ecosystem in Peru is the so-called 'integrity model and integrity function' that every public entity has to implement, regardless of the level of government. These elements were first envisioned by the Public Administration Ethics Code Law (Law 27815) of 2002 establishing that a senior management body of each public entity shall put measures in place to promote a culture of integrity, transparency, justice and public service as provided in the Code.

Later, Legislative Decree 1327 providing protection measures to those reporting misconducts (*denuncias*), established the creation of 'Offices of Institutional Integrity' (*Oficinas de integridad institutional*, or OII) as organisational units that regularly assume institutional integrity and ethics promotion in public entities. The role of the OIIs is further emphasised in the National Plan that assigns them the responsibility to implement the integrity model, which is defined as the set of processes and policies aimed at preventing corruption and other unlawful practices in an entity.

For this purpose, the OIIs should be assigned a number of responsibilities (Box 2.2) related to the articulation and monitoring of the nine elements of the model, which are:

- commitment of the senior leadership
- risk management
- integrity policies
- transparency, open data and accountability
- internal and external control and audit
- communication and training
- complaint channels
- cversight and monitoring of the integrity model
- a person in charge of the integrity model.

Box 2.2. The role of OIIs according to the National Integrity Plan

According to the National Integrity Plan and the integrity model laid out therein, the Office of Institutional Integrity (OII) shall be established with the following tasks, responsibilities and characteristics:

- The person in charge of the Integrity Model assumes the role of articulating and monitoring the components thereof.
- Depending on the size of the entity and vulnerabilities it is exposed to, the task of implementation is performed by the OII or an official who performs these functions. In cases in which the institution has an Ombudsperson, office of transparency or anti-corruption office, it could assume as well the functions of the person in charge of the Office of Institutional Integrity.
- The person in charge shall have a high-level position within the entity's organisational structure.
- Empowerment is derived from the high hierarchical level. It requires public support of senior management in the follow up function of the integrity policy.
- The functions of the person in charge shall be independent from any particular burden or interest. Therefore, the full independence of the person in charge shall be guaranteed regarding his/her actions and formulation of recommendations that he/she deems pertinent.
- It is necessary to equip the Office with the resources needed for the effective performance of his/her duties.
- The person in charge of the OII does not own the processes of the integrity model he or she shall monitor.

Source: (OECD, 2019[12]), National Plan of Integrity and Fight Against Corruption (PNILC).

The Integrity Function, in particular, the OIIs

Further guidance for the implementation of the integrity function is provided by the Secretariat for Public Integrity with Resolution No. 1-2019-PCM/SIP, which makes it mandatory for all the entities of the public administration as defined by Supreme Decree N° 054-2018-PCM, including regional and local governments (Article 1, Preliminary Title, Law No. 27444).

The Resolution describes the integrity function as the one aiming at:

- The implementation of the integrity model established in the National Plan.
- The development of mechanisms and instruments for the promotion of integrity.
- The observance and internalisation of the values and principles linked with the proper use of funds, resources, assets and public responsibilities.

More specifically, the integrity function consists of the following activities:

- Support in the identification and management of risks of corruption.
- Propose integrity and anti-corruption actions, as well as oversee its compliance.
- Propose the incorporation of integrity objectives and actions in the strategic plans of the entity.
- Implement, lead and manage the institutional integrity and anticorruption strategy, and oversee its compliance.
- Oversee compliance with regulation on transparency, asset declaration and conflicts of interest.
- Co-ordinate with the highest administrative authority and other departments the planning, execution, follow up and evaluation of the internal control system.
- Co-ordinate and implement the development of awareness-raising activities on public ethics, transparency, access to public information, asset declarations, conflict of interest, internal control and other subjects related to integrity and the fight against corruption.
- Receive, assess, channel, follow up and systematise complaints/reports on acts of corruption, ensuring the confidentiality of information.
- Provide protection measures to complainant or witness as appropriate.
- Guide and advice public officials concerning doubts, ethical dilemmas, conflict of interest situations, as well as reporting channels and protection measures and other aspects of the integrity policy.
- Monitor the implementation of the integrity model.
- Perform other ones deriving from the relevant legal framework.

While the implementation of the integrity function rests on the head of the entity, its exercise shall be either carried out by:

- the OII; or
- the highest administrative authority, which in turn may delegate it to a functional unit, permanent working group or public official belonging to such authority; or the human resources department. In Regional Governments, the highest administrative authority is the General Management Department (*Gerencia General Regional*), in Local Governments, the Municipal Management (*Gerencia Municipal*).

For the creation of an OII, this should report directly to the head of the entity or the highest administrative authority in order to ensure the high-level exposure and its adequate empowerment for the functions to be realised. Practically, the creation of an OII should be reflected in the Regulation of Organisation and Function (*Reglamento de Organización y Funciones*). The OIIs, or those exercising the integrity function, have also technical and functional relationships with the Secretariat for Public Integrity, which is the leading entity of the National Integrity Policy and may adopt mandatory regulation as well as recommendations directed to them.

The resolution for the implementation of the integrity function applies to all entities. In particular, the choice regarding the organisational arrangement is left to the entity itself in accordance with the organic structure, budget resources, level of corruption risk and number of staff members dedicated to the exercise of the integrity function. These criteria apply and guide all entities, including regional governments, and they are framed generally without any detailed elaboration.

Regional and local governments have their own structural characteristics and challenges in relation to risks, structures, capacities and budget that influences the implementation of the integrity function (see the "Challenges to implementing the Integrity Model (Modelo de Integridad) in the regions" sub-section in Chapter 2). These features could be considered more closely and granularly to provide them with specific guidance on modalities to implement the integrity function coherently with their reality (see the "Setting realistic standards for the integrity advisory function in Regional Governments" sub-section in Chapter 3).

Other relevant actors in the Regional governments for the integrity model

Regardless of the modality to put it into practice, the integrity function has a pivotal role in implementing the integrity model. However, its role is firstly to co-ordinate, monitor and verify compliance with the components of the model whose responsibilities are spread among various actors within the entity.

As illustrated in a previous OECD study (OECD, 2019[12]), the body/person in charge of the integrity function advises and supports a number of units responsible for the integrity model, which are also present in regional governments:

- General Management (*Gerencia General*).
- Technical Secretariat for the Disciplinary Administrative Process.
- Attorney General Office.
- Office of Institutional Control.
- Transparency Unit/person.
- Human Resources Office.

Current implementation of the integrity function and model in Peru's regions

While the implementation of the integrity function and model at the central level is advancing in all ministries, with all of them having one or more integrity and anti-corruption units with different institutional arrangements and functions (OECD, 2019[12]), the process is still at an early stage at the regional level for a number of both structural and contextual conditions (see the "Challenges to implementing the Integrity Model (Modelo de Integridad) in the regions" sub-section in Chapter 2). According to the information provided by the Secretariat for Public Integrity as of November 2020 only six Regional Governments – Amazonas, Cajamarca, La Libertad, Lambayeque, Piura and San Martín – have appointed the body or person in charge of the integrity function (see Annex A).

More generally, initiatives related to the various components of the model are still limited and scattered across regions. For example, as of November 2020, at the subnational level, only six Regional Governments and five municipalities had adopted a code of conduct. Efforts are on-going to adopt and implement a code of conduct in Regional Governments. The efforts are also supported by a specific programme of the Subnational Programme for Public Finances Management of the Swiss Cooperation with the contribution of the OECD that provided a methodology stressing the key concept of the public officials' participation during the entire implementation process, from the assessment of the entity's integrity context (actors, perception, regulation) to the dissemination of the code itself (Basel Institute on

Governance, 2018[13]). The programme supported 6 Regional Governments and 5 municipalities in elaborating a code in such participative matters.

In this process, the following findings and challenges have been highlighted:

- Some Regional Governments did not have reliable staff databases, which made sampling difficult.
- Some public officials were not aware of their own standards because they are not always published, although they were in force.
- Low co-ordination within Regional Governments and high turnover of public officials.
- The election period in 2018 and the renewal of regional political authorities in 2019 – at the same time as municipal ones – lead to incentives to adopt codes of conduct just before and after elections (Basel Institute of Governance, 2020[14]).

Similar support has been provided by the Swiss Cooperation, again with support from the OECD, to strengthen corruption risk management, another weak component of the integrity model at the regional level, through a methodological guide (Basel Institute on Governance, 2018[15]).

National actors and policies impacting regional integrity systems

Regional governments have the mission to promote the regional economy and development within their jurisdiction; to encourage investments, and develop activities and public services in line with national policies and national and regional development plans. Main actors in the decision-making process are: 1) the Regional Council, the regulatory and supervisory body of the Regional Government with a role close to the one of the legislative branch; and 2) the Presidency, the executive body, which are also assisted by a Council for Regional Co-ordination, a consultative body integrated by the president of the region, provincial mayors of the region (60% of the Council) and representatives of the civil society (40% of the Council). In terms of competences, the regional level of government has both exclusive and shared ones (Table 2.3).

Table 2.3. Regional Government competencies

Sector	Exclusive	Shared
Planning and budget	• Plan regional development and execute the corresponding socio-economic programmes • Formulate and approve the concerted regional development plan with the municipalities and the civil society of their region • Formulate the budget, then approved by National Government • Approve its internal organisation	
Public investments and public works	• Promote and execute regional public investments in the realms of road infrastructure, energy, communications and regional basic services. This has to be done within a framework of sustainability, competitiveness development, promotion of private investments and stimulation of markets	
Economic policies	• Design and execute regional programmes of basins, economic corridors and intermediary cities • Promote the creation of firms and regional economic units concerting productive and service provision systems • Facilitate processes oriented towards international markets for agriculture, agroindustry, craftsmanship, forestry and other productive sectors depending on potentialities • Develop touristic circuits that could become development axes • Promote the modernisation of small and medium-sized enterprises in the region, particularly articulating education, labour and technological policies	• Promotion, management and regulation of economic and productive activities in the sectors of agriculture, fishery, industry, trade, tourism, energy, oil and gas, mining, transport, communications and environment • Promote regional competitiveness and employment by co-ordinating the use of public and private resources

Sector	Exclusive	Shared
Urban planning, land property management and housing	• Develop touristic circuits that could become development axes	• Land-use planning
Environment	• Promote sustainable use of forestry resources and biodiversity	• Sustainable management of natural resources and improvement of environmental quality • Preservation and management of natural reserves and protected natural areas
Culture		• Increase accessibility and diffusion of culture and reinforce regional artistic and cultural institutions
Education		• Management of pre-school, primary, secondary and non-university tertiary educational services, taking into consideration the inter-cultural component of the region
Health		• Participation in the management of public health
Citizen participation		• Enhance and strengthen citizen participation by concerting public and private interests
Others	• Enhance and strengthen citizen participation by concerting public and private interests • Develop alliances and agreements with other regions that could foster economic, social and environmental development • Organise and approve technical cases of territorial demarcation within the region • Dictate norms on matters of their competence • Other competencies transferred by law	• Other competencies transferred by law

Source: (OECD, 2016[16]).

Coherently with Peru's decentralisation model and process, a number of national actors have both direct and indirect influence on regional governments' integrity systems and policies in terms of oversight, guidance, human resources, capacity building, co-ordination, organisational structure, and control. In order to support regional integrity, it would be vital that the national actors co-ordinate their actions to exploit synergies and avoid gaps, duplication and fragmentation (see the "Promoting an enabling environment to integrity from the national level" sub-section in Chapter 3).

Key actors with direct influence on regional integrity policies include:

- The **Secretary for Public Integrity** (*Secretaría de Integridad Publica*, SIP) in the Presidency of the Council of Ministers (PCM) is the entity that governs integrity policies in Peru. Created in April 2018 by Supreme Decree 042-2018-PCM, it is the technical body in charge of conducting and supervising compliance with the National Policy of Integrity and Fight against Corruption at both the national and subnational levels as well as of developing mechanisms and instruments to prevent and manage the risks of corruption. It is also responsible for proposing, co-ordinating, conducting, directing, supervising and evaluating policies, plans and strategies, in matters of integrity and public ethics. As governing entity for integrity, the SIP provides advice, guidance, directives, rules and technical opinions as done – for example - through guidelines for developing CRAs' anti-corruption plans and implementing the integrity function at entity level. Given the SIP's role of CAN's Technical Secretariat, it is also the co-ordinating body between the Legislative and Judicial branches, civil society, private sectors, CAN members and the Executive Branch. In such role, it also has the responsibility to co-ordinate and closely communicate with the CRAs to implement the National Integrity Policy and Plan at regional level.

- The **National Civil Service Authority** (*Autoridad Nacional del Servicio Civil*, SERVIR) in the Presidency of the Council of Ministers is the specialised technical agency and ruling body of the national human resources administration system is responsible for promoting a transparent, ethical and objective performance of civil servants. Recent programmes, initiatives and activities addressing challenges in the implementation of the integrity function at the regional level include:

  o Courses on ethics in public management as well as on ethical dilemmas developed with the National School of Public Administration.

  o An ethical survey was carried out in 2018 among more than 300 public officials of 14 regions, whose results highlight a lack of spaces for ethical reflection within the entities and that the majority of officials consider that they are not sufficiently protected when they report complaints related to unethical conduct (Box 2.6).

  o Systematisation of the information related to profiles of positions and services in regional entities in view of providing management tools tailored to their population with the objective of ordering and making more efficient the organisation structure, processes and management of human resources which currently suffers several challenges.

  o Assignment of public managers selected by SERVIR to subnational entities.

  o Technical assistance for the development of human resource management tools or for the transition to the civil service regime.

  o The Civil Service Tribunal increased focus on disputes involving subnational civil servants.

- The **Multi-sectorial Working Group** (*Grupo de Trabajo Multisectorial*) presided over by SERVIR. It was created in July 2019 and consists of other institutions such as the Secretariats for Public Management and Decentralisation, the Ministry of Economy and Finances' Directorates General for Public Human Resources and Public Budget (as members), as well as the Comptroller General Office, the National Assembly of Regional Governments and public officials from the regions (as invitees). This working group was formed to design and develop guidance and capacity-building support to improve organisational and human resources management in regional governments that would respond to challenges of such entities, thereby improving the quality of services to citizenship. In particular, specific functions entrusted in the working group according are:

  o formulating proposals for the improvement of the standards on the preparation of organisational and human resource management documents of the regional governments

  o participating in the technical discussions organised for the identification of the difficulties presented by the regional governments for organisational and human resource management

  o proposing a programme to strengthen capacities in organisational and human resource management in regional governments (Ministerial Resolution N° 268-2019-PCM).

- The **Secretariat for Decentralisation** (*Secretaría de Descentralización*), also part of the PCM, promotes and strengthens multilevel co-ordination, with the objective of narrowing information gaps and asymmetries that limit territorial development. A key on-going initiative is the creation of Regional Development Agencies (*Agencias Regionales de Desarrollo*, RDAs) with the aim of strengthening the regional economy and the social capacity of the regions through the alignment of sectoral and territorial policy priorities as well as their management and implementation through the co-ordinated intervention of the different levels of government and sectors converge (Box 2.3). In particular, their functions and objectives are:

  o to organise the co-ordinated implementation of national, sectoral and multi-sectoral policy in the territory

  o to identify and develop mechanisms to develop solutions to territorial management issues that require participation of national government entities

- ○ to identify priority policies and projects in the territory that require the participation of the executive branch and other levels of government, promoting the implementation with all relevant stakeholders
- ○ to develop mechanisms to articulate the interventions of the executive branch with regional and local governments
- ○ to provide technical assistance to regional and local governments to better perform their functions.

The RDAs are led by the regional governments and currently are being implemented in seven regions (Ayacucho, Cusco, Cajamarca, Apurímac, Piura, La Libertad y San Martín). However, over the long term, it is planned to establish them in all regions.

In this context, the Secretariat for Decentralisation also organises a series of meetings between the national executive branch and the regional governments, where Ministers engage bilaterally with the Regional Governors and their respective technical teams, to strengthen relations of trust and improve mutual understanding of their responsibilities. These meetings, called "GORE Executive" (*GORE ejecutivos*), touch upon the following thematic areas: investment unbundling, regulatory streamlining and development of regional territorial agendas (Secretaría de Descentralización, n.d.[17]).

Box 2.3. Implementing a regional approach to economic development in Peru through Regional Development Agencies

The OECD has been promoting the establishment of Regional Development Agencies (RDAs) as one option to develop the needed skills and technical capacity of Peru's regional governments based on the experience of OECD countries. In particular, the OECD recommends Peru that these agencies focus on:

- developing the skills and technical capacity of regional governments (departments) in areas such as policy development and evaluation, strategic planning, procurement, and project/programme delivery
- providing support to departments and municipal governments to better integrate strategic plans with fiscal frameworks and investment strategies
- communicating the strategic priorities of the departments to the national government, identifying opportunities for strategic alignment between departments, and ensuring these priorities inform the national budget and planning cycle
- ensuring that national policies and priorities are considered and reflected in departmental planning
- co-ordinating investments and programme delivery at a regional and inter-regional scale
- evaluating and monitoring departmental and municipal level planning to ensure plans are effective and aligned with the national system of strategic planning.

Source: (OECD, 2016[16]).

- The **Public Administration Secretariat** (*Secretaría de Gestión Pública*, or SGP) within the Presidency of the Council of Ministers is responsible for the organisation, structure and operation of the public administration, administrative simplification, management of processes, quality and attention to citizens, open government and knowledge management. It is the governing body of the National Modernisation Policy and of the Administrative System for modernising public management. One component of this system contemplates the evaluation of management risks (Supreme Decree 123-2018-PCM), which is implemented in accordance with the guidelines and methodologies defined by the SIP and the Comptroller General's Office within the framework of their respective competencies.

- The **Office of the Comptroller General** (*Contraloría General de la República*, or CGR) is the highest authority of the National Control System. It supervises, monitors and verifies the correct application of public policies and the use of public resources and assets. In order to carry out its functions efficiently, it has administrative, functional, economic and financial autonomy. The CGR is observing members of the CAN. Its competences include controlling and supervising regional governments in a decentralised and permanent manner through regional offices. These regional offices are also observing members of the CRAs. The Office also carries out continuous monitoring of the recent Directive for the implementation of the National Control System No. 006-2019-CGR/INTEG, which has different requirements for regions. In this context, 6 regions benefitted from capacity-building activities of the Basel Institute for Governance. In line with a control strategy based on prevention, the CGR has recently initiated concurrent controls integrating its traditional strategy based on preventive controls and ex-post audit activity in view of addressing the weakness of internal controls in public institutions. (Box 2.4)

Box 2.4. Concurrent control model in Peru

Starting from 2017, the Comptroller General Office of Peru started to carry out concurrent controls, supporting entities through the evaluation of a set of control milestones belonging to an ongoing process, with the purpose of verifying whether they are carried out in accordance with current regulations, internal provisions, contractual or other similar provisions that are applicable to them. At the same time, they allow to identify, if necessary, the existence of situations that affect or may affect the continuity, the result or the achievement of the objectives of the process, and communicate them in a timely manner to the entity or agency to charge of the process, so that the corresponding preventive or corrective actions are adopted (Directives N° 005-2017-CG/PROCAL and N° 002-2019-CG-NORM, approved by Comptroller's Resolution N° 405-2017-CG and N° 115-2019-CG).

According to the initial assessment by CGR, the implementation of the concurrent control model shows positive results and comparative advantages associated with the use of a multidisciplinary team that applies specialised methods (scientific and technological) related to the process being controlled. In particular, it seems to increase the possibility of breaking collusion and bribery circles through systematic supervision during the milestones that are most at risk during the execution process of a public work. Furthermore, it modifies the incentive structure of public officials and private entities for engaging in illegal behaviour as well as promotes social control and significant improvements in the transparency of control and accountability, through the full publicity of control reports.

Source: (Shack Yalta, 2019[18]).

- The **Ombudsman Office** (*Defensoría del Pueblo*) is an independent institution in charge of promoting the rights of citizens and which supervises compliance with duties of the State and oversees the performance of public services. It is a member of the CAN (with voice but no vote) and, at regional level, 28 regional offices take part in the CRAs. As part of its work on corruption, the Ombudsman Office has been monitoring the activity status of the CRAs (Defensoria del Pueblo, 2018[10]) as well as on-going criminal proceedings against public officials on corruption by department (Figure 2.2).

- The **Ministry of Justice and Human Rights** (*Ministerio de Justicia y Derechos Humanos*) is responsible, among other tasks, for guaranteeing transparency and access to information as one of its Directorate General exercises the function of National Transparency and Access to Public Information Authority (*Autoridad Nacional de Transparencia y Acceso a la Información Pública*). Within the Ministry, the Tribunal for Transparency and Access to Public Information is a decision-making body with functional independence to which one can appeal to resolve any dispute related to transparency and the right to access to public information by public entities. In these matters, regional governments are subject to a number of obligations as any other public entity, including the appointment of an official responsible for access to information and transparency-related tasks (Ministerio de Justicia y Derechos Humanos, 2019[19]). Under the Ministry of Justice, the Anticorruption Prosecutor Office (*Procuraduría Pública Especializada en Delitos de Corrupción*) exercises the legal defence of the State at national level through the exercise of procedural action, the collection of civil damages and the recovery of assets in relation to corruption offences.

- The **Attorney General's Office** (*Ministerio Público*, or MP) is a constitutionally-autonomous institution of the State whose main functions are the protection of the principle of legality, citizens' rights and public interests, the representation of the State in court, the prosecution of crime and civil reparation. The MP is made up of a range of regional and supra-regional units and offices, including units dedicated to the investigation and prosecution of corruption.

- The **Judiciary** (*Poder Judicial*) is the institution that exercises and administers justice in Peru based on the Constitution and law. While the Supreme Court of Justice has competence on the whole national territory, the Superior Courts (*Cortes Superiores*) exercise jurisdiction at the subnational level in Peru, namely in its 35 judicial districts distributed amongst the 25 Peruvian regions.

In addition, there are stakeholders of Peru's public sector that – although not being directly responsible for integrity-related matters –have an impact on regional integrity systems as they co-ordinate regional leaderships, govern key corruption risk areas or have a role in strategic public policy making. These include:

- The **National Assembly of Regional Governments** (*Asamblea Nacional de Gobiernos Regionales*, ANGR) is an organisation, composed of the governors of the 25 regional governments, that promotes good governance practices, transparency and the fight against corruption; it supports regional integration initiatives and develops proposals to advance decentralisation.

- The **Ministry of Economy and Finance**, which is responsible for formulating, proposing, executing and evaluating policies, regulations and technical guidelines relating to public procurement matter;

- The **Government Procurement Supervising Agency** (*Organismo Supervisor de las Contrataciones del Estado*, OSCE), an autonomous public entity attached to the Ministry of Economy and Finance (*Ministerio de Economía y Finanzas,* MEF) that supervises the procurement process, selectively and/or randomly verifying the procedures made by the public entities while procuring goods, services or works. In the past, the OSCE carried out a Support and Follow-up Programme (*Programa de Acompañamiento y Seguimiento*), where also some regional governments took part, that aimed at promoting the improvement of public procurement management, as well as minimising frequent errors and incompliances in the processes and developing good contracting practices. Throughout the support programme, common risks observed were limited controls to detect non-compliance with the regulations, absence of standardised documents, lack of scheduling of the contracting process, insufficient knowledge, limited number of staff in the contracting bodies with OSCE-certification, insufficient training, unclear internal organisation of roles and responsibilities, and a high number of errors in applying the procurement regulations correctly. Based on these common deficiencies, the OSCE designed a new technical assistance and monitoring programme in 2020. It focuses on priority projects at the national, regional and local level overseeing the entire procurement cycle. Weekly meetings are organised with the MEF to provide timely assistance. Technical assistance is currently provided to all twenty-four regional governments. This permanent support throughout the whole project cycle enables the identification of irregularities and integrity risks in order to mitigate them proactively.

- The **Central Purchasing Body** (*Perú Compras*, PC), which was created in 2008 – becoming operational in 2015 – to increase savings in the public procurement system by obtaining lower prices and reduced transaction costs, also in support of subnational entities and their co-ordination in purchases. (OECD, 2017[20])
- The **National Strategic Planning Centre** (CEPLAN), also integrated within the PCM, plays a co-ordinating role between the Regions and national government insofar as it is the governing, guiding and co-ordinating body of the National Strategic Planning System, promoting the development of strategic planning as a technical instrument of government and management.

Challenges to implementing the Integrity Model (*Modelo de Integridad*) in the regions

Ensuring that integrity policies at the national level are reaching effectively the subnational level is one of the most common challenges in establishing a coherent integrity system among the different levels of government. Weak or lack of vertical co-ordination mechanisms between the national and subnational level can lead to vacuums and threatening the effectiveness of the central integrity system as a whole. Therefore, as stressed by the *OECD Recommendation of the Council on Public Integrity* (OECD, 2017[21]), it is essential to establish mechanisms for co-operation that support implementation "through formal or informal means to support coherence and avoid overlap and gaps, and to share and build on lessons learned from good practices."

A strong top-down approach consisting of the central level setting policies to be implemented without assessing the specifics needs of the subnational level or asking for feedback from the subnational level, can further discourage subnational actors and make them reluctant to co-ordinate. It is necessary to find measures that will reinforce ownership among the subnational governments, as otherwise the strategy set at the national level will be perceived as an obligation and merely turned into a check the box exercise. In this regard, the national level also needs to undertake efforts to set incentives for the subnational level to strengthen integrity by rewarding the proactive generation of regional models and providing appropriate resources and by illustrating the wider benefits of integrity such as better return on investments, delivery of public goods and services, building citizen trust and similar (OECD, 2018[1]).

As such, the implementation of the integrity model and integrity function at the regional level depends on taking into account the specific capacities and opportunities for strengthening integrity at the subnational level. If the focus lies on the mere formal creation of the integrity model and integrity function, without assessing the context, capacities, resources and vulnerabilities to integrity and defining priorities and specific, concrete objectives that are relevant for the citizens (e.g. integrity in health or education), the model and function may exist on paper, but will hardly exercise the functions and achieve impact as expected, nor will it be understood, supported and hence "demanded" by citizens.

High regional diversity stresses economic differences and social disparities

The *OECD Territorial Reviews: Peru 2016* (OECD, 2016[16])carried out under the OECD Country Programme with Peru shows that the main challenges facing the country's national development stem from persistent, acute regional disparities and the over-concentration of economic activity in some territories, especially Lima, coupled with the physical isolation of other, remote regions in the south and east of the country. Coastal regions tend to have better socio-economic conditions than uplands and rainforest regions in the interior of the country. The economies of coastal regions are more diversified, with manufacturing, commerce and services activities. The uplands and rainforest regions, which are in general more rural, are resource dependent and specialise in different mineral and agricultural commodities.

The informal sector is high across all regions. For instance, the Peruvian National Institute of Statistics (*Instituto Nacional de Estadística e Informática*, INEI) reports a level of around 72% of informal employment. The relationship between corruption and informality is complex (de Soto, 1989[22]; Choi and Thum, 2005[23]; Andres and Ramlogan-Dobson, 2011[24]), but operating in the informal sector typically result in specific corruption risks, such as bribery and extortion related to inspections in the public space or in relation to business licences. Regions may also be affected to a different degree by illegal economic activities, such as illegal mining or logging that are often related to organised crime. For example, drug-related organised crime activities are related to the areas of production and access to ports or borders from which the drugs can be exported. Lastly, illegal activities around prostitution may exist everywhere but could be concentrated in certain areas, especially in areas of small-scale and illegal mining. All these illegal activities have in common that they typically use corrupt practices to operate and turn a blind eye on prosecution. As such, the extend of illegal activities will impact significantly on the types and extend of corrupt practices in a given region.

Within these broader patterns, each region has its own particular socio-economic and ecological features, which has its distinct vulnerabilities to corruption (OECD, 2016[16]). This diversity challenges the assertion of implementing a one-size-fits-all model. Instead, the specific context should be taken into account when developing an approach to strengthen integrity at the subnational level.

Decentralisation is a work in progress

Decentralisation can address the issue of large-scale distrust in the government. With empowerment at the subnational level, citizens potentially can become involved in the deliberative processes, while public officials can be held accountable for the end results and benefits of their actions. However, a lack of integrity at the subnational level is a major risk for the decentralisation reforms as they lead to a transfer of resources and decision-making power.

Since 2002, Peru has advanced in terms of political and administrative decentralisation, with the election of regional governments and the transfer of significant responsibilities to the subnational level. However, the process is ongoing, with fiscal decentralisation remaining limited, as well as the degree of decision-making autonomy.

For example, regional Governors have decision powers related, for instance, to the planning and execution of socio-economic projects and promoting and implementing regional public investments in road, energy, communication and basic services infrastructure projects. But the governors still rely on approval from the central level for many key decisions. Similarly, the process has not been accompanied by fiscal decentralisation measures such as changes to tax and transfer arrangements. Lastly, there is no coherent strategy to increase skills, capabilities and oversight at the subnational level thereby affecting the implementation and operationalisation of the National Integrity Policy at the regional level.

This situation, coupled with overlapping responsibilities and competencies between levels of government and limited levels of horizontal and vertical co-ordination, has prevented the country from gaining the benefits associated with decentralisation (OECD, 2016[16]). Mainstreaming integrity throughout decentralisation policies helps to strengthen institutional capacities, which in turn contribute to effective policy implementation. At the same time, it is crucial to address the challenges in the decentralisation process (Box 2.5), as they hinder the effective implementation of national policies (including on integrity.

Box 2.5. Peru's key decentralisation challenges

Peru has come a long way in certain aspects of its decentralisation process. The levels of competencies and expenditure responsibilities of subnational governments are in many aspects similar to those of OECD countries.

Despite the progress in recent years, an OECD report from 2016 (OECD, 2016[16]) highlighted how certain features of Peru´s decentralisation process were limiting its possibility to unleash the full potential of decentralisation overall:

- Competences and responsibilities are not clearly defined between the levels of government.
- Within the decentralisation framework, there are several overlaps in competencies as well as a limited definition of the particular responsibilities assigned to each level of government.
- There is a misalignment between responsibilities allocated to subnational governments and the resources and capabilities available to them, which generates a systemic problem in relation to the inability to properly execute tasks and responsibilities, lack of accountability for outcomes and can leave subnational governments highly dependent on national level transfers.
- The decentralisation process was too quick in transferring responsibilities to subnational governments that did not necessarily have the human and institutional capacity to take on those responsibilities.
- There is a lack of effective mechanisms and incentives to co-ordinate policies and investments at a subnational level. These co-ordination failures appear at all levels of government, both horizontally and vertically.
- Policies are delivered on a sectoral basis with actions that may contradict one another at the local level. Co-ordination, rather than fragmentation, is a more binding constraint in relation to the delivery of better public policy outcomes.
- Subnational governments strongly depend upon transfers as a source of income. Transfers are mostly earmarked or consist of deconcentrated expenditures, limiting the autonomy of subnational governments, and particularly regional governments, to adapt policies to local needs and circumstances.
- There are limited incentives and capacity to develop tax revenues at a subnational level. Revenues of subnational governments strongly fluctuate and the central government has a certain degree of discretion in the allocation of resources. Subnational tax revenues are important in decentralised countries to improve policy outcomes, improve expenditure efficiency and accountability.
- The distributional system of the fiscal income from extractive industries (or the *canon* in Spanish) is designed to primarily compensate producing regions for the depletion of natural capital.
- The absence of stabilisation and equalisation funds has generated significant vertical and horizontal fiscal imbalances and inequalities between regions.
- The lack of effective integration between planning and resource allocation, and programme-based budgeting instruments coupled with a misalignment of incentives (political and administrative) has led to the production of suboptimal and fragmented investments. This is exacerbated by the prominent role of municipalities in allocating funds from mining royalties (the canon).
- The delivery and administration of policies, planning and regulatory instruments, and investments are not consistently monitored and evaluated at a subnational level.

- Public policies are not consistently implemented and there is a wide variety of performance between different subnational governments.
- The skills and capabilities of the public sector at a subnational level are generally low, and there is a lack of coherent strategy to address this issue.

Source: (OECD, 2016[16]).

Political leadership and senior civil servants have a low degree of ownership for integrity

One of the key principles set out in the *OECD Recommendation of the Council on Public Integrity* and the Peruvian Integrity Model is the commitment and leadership by the top-level management. Leaders are expected to be effective public managers, capable of steering their teams, inspiring their workforce, and setting an organisational culture that promotes innovation while reinforcing public sector values, including high standards for integrity and ethics.

In light of these responsibilities, leaders' roles in promoting and actively managing integrity in their organisations cannot be underestimated. Leaders assign resources to integrity systems, designate them as organisational priorities, oversee their co-ordination and integrate them into the core of their organisational management. Without committed leadership, integrity systems cannot deliver their intended impact. Moreover, by setting a personal example, leaders are a core ingredient to establish and reinforce an integrity culture in public sector organisations (OECD, 2020[25]).

Political will at the subnational level responds to its own incentives with specific dynamics of power that crucially depend on the decentralisation arrangements as well as the gaps and inconsistencies in the implementation of the desired model. (Box 2.5) In Peru, for example, the formal attribution of powers to subnational entities is inconsistent with the fact that key decisions are taken at the central level in aspects such as budget definition and allocation. In this context, reform incentives and the "business case" for integrity tend to be formulated nationally, as it has been the case for the integrity model and functions. However, winners and losers of reform are also found at the subnational level, and the subnational government authority political calculus has little to do with incentives for reform at the national level, and instead are directly connected with its immediate context such as the regional political cycle or the demand from Regional Council and local civil society.

Interview in preparation for this report revealed that the majority of the senior leadership at the regional leadership have a limited awareness of the benefits and reach of the integrity model and functions. As such, they have and perceive very limited incentives to embark on integrity reforms other than complying with the obligations set at the national level. Furthermore, the term limit for governors may generate limitations in the capacity and willingness to embark on long-term integrity reform and for building on integrity reforms undertaken by previous officeholders.

Ensuring integrity in regional politics

Participating in public life and influencing public policies are fundamental rights in a democracy. Inclusive public policies and decision making based on integrity, participation and transparency legitimise and make policies more effective, building citizens' trust in their governments (OECD, 2017[26]). However, powerful individuals and interest groups can use their wealth, power or advantages to tip the scale in their favour at the expense of the public interest. When public policy decisions are consistently or repeatedly directed away from the public interest towards the interests of a specific interest group or person, policies are captured.

As emphasised in the *OECD Integrity Review of Peru*, the risk of policy capture through the funding of political parties and election campaigns is perceived as prevalent in Peru (OECD, 2017[6]). In particular, challenges emerge in relation to private funding, especially in the form of contributions that are then repaid by assigning public contracts and that in some cases come from dubious sources such as persons likely linked to illegal economies and organisations. One example mentioned in that study that is relevant for the regional context suggests that some powerful private sector organisations in the extractive industries have direct access to senior government officials and exert influence over the public decision-making process through a number of channels, most notably through the funding of political parties and election campaigns.

Furthermore, the integrity of regional politics is undermined by the weakness of local political parties and the emergence, in parallel, of short-lived regional movements consisting of "coalitions of independent candidates" (*coaliciones de independientes*). These movements favoured the emergence of candidates who had resources and visibility to finance and support their own campaign. These dynamics also have led to regional policies often aiming at short-term benefits and weakened political discussion on strategic issues such as territorial development. The coalitions further led to the disappearance of parties' accountability mechanisms. At the same time, this situation has promoted the success of *caudillos* creating parties based on clientelism and patronage (Mujica, Melgar and Zevallos Trigoso, 2017[27]; Vega Luna et al., 2018[28]).

Budget constraints undermine the effective implementation of integrity policies and measures

Among the challenges posed by decentralisation, there is a mismatch between the spending responsibilities assigned to the regional governments and their revenues. Currently, responsibilities transferred to subnational governments are mostly financed by national government transfers. Regions have no taxing capacity, in contrast with provincial and district municipalities. As such, and confirmed by the OECD interviews held in preparation for this report, many regional governments perform their functions in the context of limited budgets. The majority of the expenditures of regional and local governments is spent on staff expenditures (in 2019, 38.5%).

Experience among OECD countries proves that in order to fully implement the functions generally associated with an Integrity Unit, adequate resources need to be assigned (OECD, 2019[12]). However, in a context of limited financial resources, it will be challenging for regional governments to assign the necessary budget to ensure a fully functioning integrity function.

A high degree of staff turnover hinders the development of capacities

Human resources management and workforce planning in subnational governments, notably to attract and retain a critical mass of well-trained, highly competent civil servants in regional administrations, are key to improving integrity. In Peru, as in OECD countries, building sufficient capacity and professionalism in subnational government is central to ensuring that they are able to meet their responsibilities and contribute to a culture of integrity. The incomplete decentralisation process in Peru is however also reflected in low salaries and in the weak institutional capacity and organisation in many of its regions. As a result, challenges in human resources present at the national level are magnified at the regional level (OECD, 2016[29]; OECD, 2017[6]).

Peru's subnational governments appear to be facing, to a large extent, similar challenges and opportunities to enhance the capacity and capability of their internal workforce. In 2018, 55% of Peruvian public sector employees are located at the subnational level (42% at the regional level and 13% at the municipal level) and approximately 45% at the national level, excluding public employees working for the judiciary, the legislative or constitutionally autonomous bodies (*Organismos Constitucionales Autónomos*).

The OECD interviews in three selected regions confirmed that with every change in political mandate, the regions experience an extensive staff turnover in their public administrations. While the discretion to recruit and dismiss regional staff by local authorities is part of the decentralisation process, it entails risks for the stability and professionalism of the workforce. An assessment of the civil service knowledge of SERVIR identified generally low knowledge of public servants in the areas of public budget, and public management and modernisation. In addition, knowledge among civil servants is higher in Lima than in the rest of the regions, and particularly with the more isolated regions, the East, where the state is less present (Box 2.6)

To address these risks, starting from 2020 the human resources department of national and regional entities need to illustrate the needs and request a favourable opinion from SERVIR prior to contracting according to the Administrative Services Contract's regime (*Contrato Administrativo de Servicios*, CAS) (SERVIR Resolution 168-2019-SERVIR-PE). In this context, SERVIR should advance the plan to set up a digital platform to track HR processes across the country, which could also play an effective role in ensuring meritocracy and mitigating some of the integrity risks in the contracting of personnel at the regional level. As pointed out in the OECD Integrity Review, when effective controls and safeguards are not in place, this can create opportunities for corrupt employment practices (OECD, 2017[6]) and undermines the capacities and knowledge of the civil service (OECD, 2016[29]). In this respect, SERVIR has been working on the design of an HR platform (*Plataforma del Portal Talento Perú*) since July 2020 and plans to launch the first version in December 2020 featuring the processes related to hiring and renewing contracts, with the aim to progressively integrate all other processes of the Human Resource Management Administrative System (*Sistema Administrativo de Gestión de Recursos Humanos*).

Figure 2.6. Peruvian civil service knowledge of public budget, and public management and modernisation

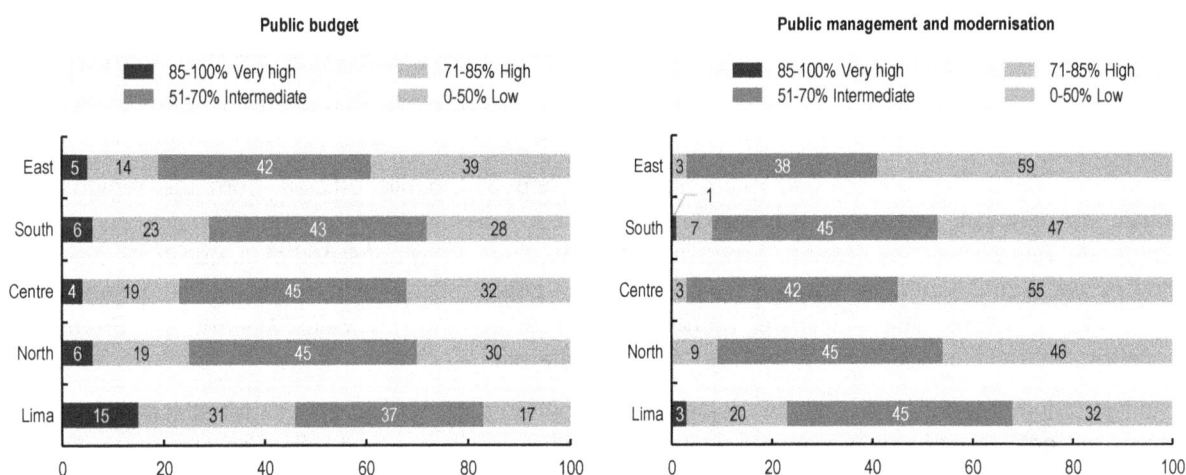

Source: (OECD, 2016[29]), based on information provided by SERVIR.

Supporting the implementation of integrity within the government, requires public servants who have a specific knowledge of integrity and anti-corruption measures and experience in promoting these throughout the public administration. According to a perception survey conducted by SERVIR in 14 regional entities, this is a challenge in Peru where the majority of interviewed officials (63%) have declared not to have attended any ethics-related activity (Box 2.6).

Given the limited degree of overall capacities and knowledge of the civil service, coupled with a high degree of rotation, the process of recruiting civil servants capable of fulfiling the integrity function could prove difficult. Similarly, a high degree of turnover within the integrity function hinders the effective implementation of integrity policies. In order to adequately fulfil the mandate, the civil servants responsible for integrity need to possess a good knowledge of the processes, previous measures and overall strategy for strengthening integrity in the regional government. In this way, long-term and forward-looking strategies could be implemented (OECD, 2016[29]).

It is, therefore, essential to ensure measures to attract and retain a more professional and well-prepared staff at the subnational level – including through adequate contractual arrangements and competitive compensation schemes - to guarantee a degree of administrative stability and avoid the transfer of more skilful officials to national entities (so called brain-drain). In addition, efforts should be made to ensure meritocracy processes and mitigate the risk of high staff turnover within the integrity function. This contributes to ensuring a good transition and that administrative procedures and management are stable and sustainable beyond a single electoral mandate (OECD, 2016[29]).

In this context, SERVIR and the Decentralisation and Public Management Secretariats also play a key role in so far as they support capacity building for recruitment procedures, but also train subnational public employees. The co-ordination with the SIP regarding integrity in human resources is essential. In turn, both the fairness of the process and the possibility of growing professionally at the local level may be incentives for public officials to consider the development of their careers in regional or municipal governments.

Low degree of integrity policy implementation

Overall, the implementation of integrity policies at the regional level, in particular those connected to the various components of the model, are still limited and scattered across regions. As detailed above the implementation of codes of conduct has been limited throughout the regions (see the "The implementation of the integrity model and function in the regions" sub-section in Chapter 2). The results of a survey on ethical climate among regional officials conducted by SERVIR pointed towards – among other findings –a perception of a low degree of implementation and application of the conflict of interest and whistleblowing policies (Box 2.6).

Box 2.6. SERVIR's survey of regional public officials' perceptions of the ethical climate

Throughout 2018, SERVIR carried out a survey among 317 public officials from the regions of Amazonas, Ancash, Arequipa, Cajamarca, Cusco, La Libertad, Lambayeque, Madre de Dios, Moquegua, Piura, Puno, San Martin, Tacna and Tumbes. The survey consisted of 30 questions divided into five blocks that sought to measure the perception of public officials with respect to five dimensions of the public entities' ethical climate, namely: (i) Ethical training; (ii) Value system; (iii) Strategic management; (iv) Corruption risks; and (v) Conflict of interest.

Findings of the report include that the majority of respondents do not find spaces for ethical reflection within their entities and would welcome such opportunities to discuss and reflect on ethical issues or dilemmas or ethical issues. The report also pointed out the need to further implement the integrity function in public entities since 80% of respondents declared that there is no area in charge of integrity in their entity. Weakness in the "openness" of regional entities' organisational culture emerges from the results that public officials consider not reporting possible misconducts as the safest option not to get into trouble. Similarly, the majority of public officials are not aware of the process for reporting cases of corruption and misconduct and feel that there is no sufficient protection for those who choose to report. The conflict of interest policy is also perceived as not applied in practice by leadership as there is a widespread perception that gifts or other favours are given more often to senior management than to other public officials. In terms of risk areas, the highest one identified by respondents is by far public procurement (76%), followed by the granting of permits and licenses (11%).

Source: (SERVIR, 2020[30]).

With regards to conflict of interests, interviews held in preparation for this report confirmed that there is very limited knowledge among civil servants at the regional level on their management. So far, there have been no efforts made by regional governments to implement awareness-raising campaigns on how to identify and manage conflict-of-interest situations. This leads in many cases to an environment in which instead of proactively identifying a conflict-of-interest situation, public servants will not come forward out of fear of having committed a corrupt act.

Concerning whistleblower protection, the provisions of the whistleblower protection instruments (Law No. 29542 and Legislative Decree 1327) have not been implemented effectively and there is no strategy for communicating about it or evaluating results. In the majority of cases at the subnational level, government actors will be more intimately connected to the citizens. An effective strategy to implement a whistleblower policy needs to recognise that the close proximity of the whistleblowers to the corrupt actors may increase the risk of retaliation. Accordingly, the possibility of anonymity and protection from retaliatory actions are potentially even more important at this level. While some regions have implemented a mobile app to facilitate reporting or – as in the case of Lambayeque – have provided the possibility to request protection, major constraints are the limited protections available for public servants who have reported misconduct. Coupled with low trust in the procedures, this discourages potential whistleblowers from coming forward.

References

Andres, A. and C. Ramlogan-Dobson (2011), "Is Corruption really bad for inequality? evidence from Latin America", *Journal of Development Studies*, Vol. 47/7, pp. 959-976, http://dx.doi.org/10.1080/00220388.2010.509784. [24]

Basel Institute of Governance (2020), *Resumen sobre la experiencia con Códigos de Conducta Participativos*. [14]

Basel Institute on Governance (2018), *Gestión de riesgos para la prevención de corrupción en el Perú*, http://gfpsubnacional.pe/wp-content/uploads/2018/12/Gesti%C3%B3n-de-riesgos_final.pdf. [15]

Basel Institute on Governance (2018), *Guía para la implementación participativa de un Código de Conducta*, http://gfpsubnacional.pe/wp-content/uploads/2018/12/Fortaleciendo-la-Gesti%C3%B3n-Descentraliza_final.pdf. [13]

CAN (2016), *Lineamientos para la creación de Comisiones Regionales Anticorrupción*, Comisión de Alto Nivel Anticorrupción, https://can.pcm.gob.pe/wp-content/uploads/2016/07/Lineamientos-creaci%c3%b3n-de-Comisiones-Regionales-Anticorrupci%c3%b3n.pdf. [9]

CAN (2015), *Guía para la formulación de planes regionales anticorrupción pasos y cronograma*, Comisión de Alto Nivel Anticorrupción, https://can.pcm.gob.pe/wp-content/uploads/2015/08/GUIA-PARA-LA-FORMULACION-DE-PLANES-REGIONALES-ANTICORRUPCION.pdf. [11]

Choi, J. and M. Thum (2005), "Corruption and the Shadow Economy", *International Economic Review*, Vol. 46/3, pp. 817-836, http://dx.doi.org/10.1111/j.1468-2354.2005.00347.x (accessed on 29 December 2014). [23]

Comisión Presidencial de Integridad (2017), *Informe de la Comisión Presidencial de Integridad*, https://plataformaanticorrupcion.pe/wp-content/uploads/2017/07/Informe-Final-Comision-Presidencial-de-Integridad.pdf (accessed on 4 May 2020). [7]

de Soto, H. (1989), *The Other Path: The Invisible Revolution in the Third World*, Harper & Row. [22]

Defensoria del Pueblo (2018), "Comisiones Regionales Anticorrupción: Diagnóstico y recomendaciones para mejorar su funcionamiento", *Boletín: Supervisión de Espacios Anticorrupción, Diciembre 2018 - Año I - №2*, https://www.defensoria.gob.pe/wp-content/uploads/2018/12/BOLETIN-ANTICURRUPCION.pdf (accessed on 12 June 2020). [10]

Defensoría del Pueblo (2019), *Mapas de casos de corrupción de funcionarios en trámite por departamento en el 2016 y 2018*, https://www.defensoria.gob.pe/wp-content/uploads/2019/05/Mapas-de-la-Corrupci%C3%B3n-Nro.-1-Mayo-actualizado-FINAL.pdf (accessed on 6 February 2020). [8]

Ministerio de Justicia y Derechos Humanos (2019), *Obligaciones de los gobiernos regionales y locales en materia de transparencia y acceso a la información pública*, https://www.minjus.gob.pe/wp-content/uploads/2020/02/CARTILLA_OBLIGACIONES.pdf (accessed on 2 June 2020). [19]

Mujica, J., S. Melgar and N. Zevallos Trigoso (2017), "Corrupción en gobiernos subnacionales en el Perú: Un estudio desde el enfoque de la oportunidad delictiva.", *Elecciones*, Vol. 16/17, https://dialnet.unirioja.es/servlet/articulo?codigo=6783383 (accessed on 5 June 2020). [27]

OECD (2020), *OECD Public Integrity Handbook*, OECD Publishing, Paris, https://dx.doi.org/10.1787/ac8ed8e8-en. [25]

OECD (2019), *Offices of Institutional Integrity in Peru: Implementing the Integrity System*, OECD, Paris, http://www.oecd.org/gov/ethics/offices-of-institutional-integrity-peru.pdf. [12]

OECD (2018), *Integrity for Good Governance in Latin America and the Caribbean: From Commitments to Action*, OECD Publishing, Paris, https://dx.doi.org/10.1787/9789264201866-en. [1]

OECD (2017), *Government at a Glance 2017*, OECD Publishing, Paris, http://dx.doi.org/10.1787/gov_glance-2017-en. [3]

OECD (2017), *OECD Integrity Review of Coahuila, Mexico: Restoring Trust through an Integrity System*, OECD Public Governance Reviews, OECD Publishing, Paris, http://dx.doi.org/10.1787/9789264283091-en. [2]

OECD (2017), *OECD Integrity Review of Peru: Enhancing Public Sector Integrity for Inclusive Growth*, OECD Public Governance Reviews, OECD Publishing, Paris, https://dx.doi.org/10.1787/9789264271029-en. [6]

OECD (2017), *OECD Recommendation of the Council on Public Integrity*, OECD/LEGAL/0435, https://legalinstruments.oecd.org/en/instruments/OECD-LEGAL-0435. [21]

OECD (2017), *Preventing Policy Capture: Integrity in Public Decision Making*, OECD Public Governance Reviews, OECD Publishing, Paris, https://dx.doi.org/10.1787/9789264065239-en. [26]

OECD (2017), *Public Procurement in Peru: Reinforcing Capacity and Co-ordination*, OECD Public Governance Reviews, OECD Publishing, Paris, https://dx.doi.org/10.1787/9789264278905-en. [20]

OECD (2016), *OECD Public Governance Reviews: Peru: Integrated Governance for Inclusive Growth*, OECD Public Governance Reviews, OECD Publishing, Paris, https://dx.doi.org/10.1787/9789264265172-en. [29]

OECD (2016), *OECD Territorial Reviews: Peru 2016*, OECD Territorial Reviews, OECD Publishing, Paris, https://dx.doi.org/10.1787/9789264262904-en. [16]

Procuraduría Pública Especializada en Delitos de Corrupción (2017), *Sospecha generalizada de corrupción contra gobernadores y alcaldes del país*, https://plataformaanticorrupcion.pe/wp-content/uploads/2017/07/INFORME-CORRUPCION-SOBRE-GOBERNADORES-Y-ALCALDES.pdf (accessed on 6 November 2020). [5]

Proética (2019), *XI Encuesta Nacional Anual Sobre Percepciones de Corrupción*, https://www.proetica.org.pe/contenido/xi-encuesta-nacional-sobre-percepciones-de-la-corrupcion-en-el-peru-2019/ (accessed on 25 May 2020). [4]

Secretaría de Descentralización (n.d.), *Objetivos y Funciones | Portal de la Secretaría de Descentralización*, https://www.descentralizacion.gob.pe/index.php/objetivos-y-funciones/ (accessed on 3 February 2020). [17]

SERVIR (2020), *Estudio de percepciones de los servidores civiles sobre el clima ético de sus entidades públicas*, https://storage.servir.gob.pe/servicio-civil/clima-etico-2019.pdf (accessed on 4 May 2020). [30]

Shack Yalta, N. (2019), *Concurrent Control Model as the Driving Core of a Preventive, Prompt and Timely Approach to Government Control in Peru*. [18]

Vega Luna, E. et al. (2018), *El Círculo de la Corrupción en los Gobiernos Regionales. Los casos de Cusco, Ayacucho, Moquegua, Piura y Madre de Dios*, https://www.kas.de/c/document_library/get_file?uuid=b8c8e02a-a788-91b0-3d21-3b6515f3f550&groupId=252038. [28]

3 A strategic approach towards supporting integrity in the Peruvian regions

To establish regional integrity systems, the Peruvian regional governments could implement a tailored and incremental approach, driven by the integrity function and based on available capacities, responding to main integrity risks and to a number of priority areas to which integrity policies should be applied. In addition, this integrity function could empower and improve the sustainability of the Regional Anticorruption Commissions (CRAs) as wel as serve as the link between the regional government and other integrity actors at the regional and the national level. The regional integrity function could be strengthened and supported by the Secretariat of Public Integrity and a number of other national actors, by providing strategic direction and assistance, mobilising high-level commitment, building technical capacities and promoting dialogues across regions.

The challenges at regional level outlined in Chapter 2 call for the development of a strategic approach that supports the promotion of public integrity in the regional governments. Such a strategic approach should take into consideration the regional reality and in particular the available capacities and the prevailing integrity risks. As such, regional governments could focus on a number of key integrity-related priorities to generate greater impact. In addition, the integrity function within regional government could leverage the role of the Regional Anticorruption Commission and support their work. Finally, various actors at the national level can directly or indirectly contribute to promoting an environment conducive to public integrity in the regions. In particular, the SIP has a key role in directly supporting regional efforts on public integrity while ensuring a close co-ordination and coherence with the contribution of other relevant actors such as the CAN and PCM.

Setting realistic standards for the integrity advisory function in Regional Governments

Aligning the mandate, functions and characteristics of the integrity functions to the regional realities

All public entities have a legal obligation to implement the integrity function (see the "The implementation of the integrity model and function in the regions" sub-section in Chapter 2). However, Peru's regional governments would benefit from an incremental approach that aims at a gradual implementation and develops along a number of local priorities and risks. This should also take into account the challenges of both contingent and structural nature encountered by regional governments.

If the integrity model were to be implemented at the same time and to the full extent in all regions, it would most likely merely exist on paper in many regions without fulfiling its mandate or generating impact due to limits in regional government capacities and resources. In turn, this could create cynicism among public officials and the public in general, questioning the commitment of integrity reforms and undermining the support for ongoing and future reforms. As mentioned, currently only five Regional Governments (Amazonas, Cajamarca, La Libertad, Lambayeque, Piura) have established an integrity function so far (Annex A1Part IAnnex A); and only one has a proven track of past activities and a planned strategy.

While both the National Plan and Resolution of the SIP No. 1-2019-PCM/SIP already provide for a range of options to institutionalise the integrity function, the reality at the regional level requires even more tailored – and flexible – guidance for the function's design and implementation. As discussed in the "Challenges to implementing the Integrity Model (*Modelo de Integridad*) in the regions" sub-section in Chapter 2, several challenges encountered by regional governments justify such a differentiated approach. This should also include guidance provided at the national level.

Such a differentiated approach could take account of the gap between regional and central level institutions in terms of size, which may also serve as a proxy for the level of institutional capacities, available resources and support needed. At the same time, the approach should provide a range of options that are capable to tailor the integrity function to Peru's diverse regional realities (economic but also political and geographical) as well as to the related exogenous or environmental integrity risk levels and typologies of each region. These two main dimensions, size and the level of corruption risks, are also referred to in the National Integrity Plan (Box 2.2) and Resolution No. 1-2019-PCM/SIP (Article 6.5.2). As such, an indicative matrix to guide the policies and implementation guidance by the SIP is proposed to categorise regions along these two dimensions (Table 3.1).

Table 3.1. Categorisation of regions by risk/size

Size	Risk		
	Low	Medium	High
Small	1	2	2
Medium	2	3	3
Large	2	3	4

The detailed methodology to select the relevant criteria, identify reliable sources of information and develop indicators to operationalise and measure the two dimensions should be developed, steered and owned by the SIP in dialogue and agreement with the regions. The matrix could be adopted by the CAN to institutionalise and build legitimacy of the integrity function within the regions. In support of this process, the SIP could consider a number of criteria, some of which have been pointed out by representatives of regional governments during a validation workshop held in September 2020 (Table 3.2).

Table 3.2. Proposed criteria to classify Peru's regions by size and integrity/corruption risk

Size	Integrity/Corruption Risk
• per capita income • number of staff • size of the budget • transfer from central government	• exposure to at-risk economic activities and sectors such as mining and extraction of natural resources • staff turnover rate and contractual/remuneration regime percentage of direct awards and low amounts processes (*menor cuantía*) in public procurement • incidence of organised crimes groups activities or other illicit activities • results from corruption perception and victimisation surveys • performance of regional governments in relation to the Integrity Model • resources used for consultancies • citizens perception on regional government management from the National Institute of Statistics and Informatics' report on citizen perception of governance, democracy and trust in institutions • CGR's estimated cost of corruption and functional misconduct

Source: (Shack, Pérez and Portugal, 2020[1]); (Instituto Nacional de Estadística e Informática, 2020[2]).

The institutional setup and the list of functions – among the ones defined in Resolution No. 1-2019-PCM/SIP – that could be considered as minimum requirements to implement the integrity function should be then based on the category assigned to a region by the matrix (Table 3.3). Each category would be thus the starting point to incrementally implement the full integrity function within the regional government, which – as a minimum – should focus on tasks related to the risk assessment, integrity policy and monitoring of the integrity model's implementation. In addition, a number of priority areas of application, such as mining, health, education or infrastructure, for example, should be defined based on the assessment of local risks and weaknesses.

As for the institutional setup, although the establishment of an OII is the ideal arrangement to take the key role within regional government and the ultimate objective for any entity, it is considered that the alternatives provided by the legal framework could equally serve the purpose in contexts of very limited resources, which is a reality in many regions of Peru. Any alternative set up would require direct reporting to the Governor or the highest administrative authority (and the SIP).

Such an approach for Regional Governments aligns with the guidance and criteria established in Resolution No. 1-2019-PCM/SIP, bringing the function ever closer to regional realities and enabling the incremental implementation of the function with due consideration of the challenges previously identified and guided by the matrix (see the "Challenges to implementing the Integrity Model (Modelo de Integridad) in the regions" sub-section in Chapter 2 and Table 3.1).

Table 3.3. Recommended institutional arrangements and tasks for regional integrity functions by category of risk/size

	Category of region according to the matrix			
	1	**2**	**3**	**4**
Typology of institutional arrangements (minimum)	Functional unit or permanent task force to the highest administrative authority or human resources department (upon delegation).\	Functional unit or permanent task force to the highest administrative authority or human resources department (upon delegation).	OII (2-3 persons) reporting to the highest administrative authority	OII (4-X persons) reporting to the highest administrative authority
Tasks to be performed (minimum)	• Support in the identification and management of risks of corruption (2) • Propose integrity and anticorruption actions, as well as oversee compliance (3) • Propose the incorporation of integrity objectives and actions in the strategic plans and budget of the entity (1/3) • If given the responsibilities to receive complaints/reports on acts of corruption, transfer to competent bodies, follow up and systematise them, ensuring the confidentiality of information (7) • Monitor the incremental implementation of the integrity model (8)	• Support in the identification and management of risks of corruption (2) • Propose integrity and anticorruption actions, as well as oversee compliance (3) • Propose the incorporation of integrity objectives and actions in the strategic plans and budget of the entity(1/3) • Monitor the incremental implementation of the integrity model (8) • Implement, lead and manage the institutional integrity and anticorruption strategy, and oversee its compliance (3) • Co-ordinate with the highest administrative authority and other departments the planning, execution, follow up and evaluation of the internal control system (5) • If given the responsibilities to receive complaints/reports on acts of corruption, transfer to competent bodies, follow up and systematise them, ensuring the confidentiality of information (7) • Guide and advise public officials concerning doubts, ethical dilemmas, conflict of interest situations, as well as reporting channels and protection measures and other aspects of the integrity policy (7)	• Support in the identification and management of risks of corruption (2) • Propose integrity and anticorruption actions, as well as oversee compliance (3) • Propose the incorporation of integrity objectives and actions in the strategic plans and budget of the entity (1/3) • Monitor the incremental implementation of the integrity model (8) • Implement, lead and manage the institutional integrity and anticorruption strategy, and oversee its compliance (3) • Co-ordinate with the highest administrative authority and other departments the planning, execution, follow up and evaluation of the internal control system (5) • Co-ordinate and implement the development of awareness-raising activities on public ethics, transparency, access to public information, asset declarations, conflict of interest, internal control and other subjects related to integrity and the fight against corruption (6) • If given the responsibilities to receive complaints/reports on acts of corruption, transfer to competent bodies, follow up and systematise them, ensuring the confidentiality of information (7) • Guide and advise public officials concerning doubts, ethical dilemmas, conflict of interest situations, as	• Support in the identification and management of risks of corruption (2) • Propose integrity and anticorruption actions, as well as oversee compliance (3) • Propose the incorporation of integrity objectives and actions in the strategic plans and budget of the entity (1/3) • Implement, lead and manage the institutional integrity and anticorruption strategy, and oversee its compliance (3) • Oversee compliance with regulation on transparency, asset declaration and conflicts of interest (4) • Co-ordinate with the highest administrative authority and other departments the planning, execution, follow up and evaluation of the internal control system (5) • Co-ordinate and implement the development of awareness-raising activities on public ethics, transparency, access to public information, asset declarations, conflict of interest, internal control and other subjects related to integrity and the fight against corruption (6) • If given the responsibilities to receive complaints/reports on acts of corruption, transfer to competent bodies, follow up and systematise them, ensuring the confidentiality of information (7) • Provide protection measures to complainant or witness as appropriate (7) • Guide and advise public officials concerning doubts, ethical dilemmas, conflict of interest situations, as well as reporting channels and protection measures and other aspects of the integrity policy (7) • Monitor the implementation of the integrity model (8)

Category of region according to the matrix			
1	2	3	4
		well as reporting channels and protection measures and other aspects of the integrity policy (7)	

Note: The numbers next to the tasks refer to the component number of the integrity model (see the "The implementation of the integrity model and function in the regions" sub-section in Chapter 2) they correspond to. As part of the complaints' component of the integrity model, the integrity function may be given the role of receiving complaints. If so, the task of the integrity function would consist of transferring them to the relevant actors (e.g. Technical Secretariat for the Disciplinary Administrative Process; Attorney General Office; Office of Institutional Control) and ensure the follow-up, rather than processing them. As highlighted in (OECD, 2019[3]), the processing and investigation of complaints requires substantial resources and would go beyond the preventive role the integrity function is entrusted with in the entity.

Setting priorities based on regional risks and weaknesses

In parallel to the establishment of the integrity model and to ensure setting the foundations for an integrity system in the regions, the regional governments – in co-ordination with the SIP – could identify priorities based on a diagnostic tool assessing the internal strengths and weaknesses and external opportunities and threats of the regional government (also known as SWOT-analysis). A key input for this diagnostic – but not the only one – would be the detailed integrity risk assessment carried out by the integrity function. Priorities could also be defined by taking into account the progress in the implementation of the Integrity Model measured by the Public Integrity Index, which is being developed by SIP and will represent the key input for the entity's work plan or integrity programme. At the same time, they could be defined by considering those public services delivery areas – or even specific services and objectives thereof – which can be considered as most significant in improving living conditions, such as those contributing to the achievement of the Sustainable Development Goals, and are most affected by corruption. Similarly, in order to create buy-in and support from stakeholders, the diagnostic could identify areas/sectors in which it is most likely to show tangible results or "quick wins" of strengthening integrity.

Building on the diagnostic, subnational governments – under the leadership of the integrity function's responsible official or area – should identify the priorities for strengthening integrity, determine the entity or unit responsible for defining a plan to implement such priorities and develop indicators to monitor advances in that area. In this way, subnational governments could develop a comprehensive integrity strategy – while ensuring the availability of appropriate budget resources – which would examine on a regular basis the progress made to ensure that the limited resources and capacities are used in the most efficient manner.

Regarding the specific priority areas, experience has shown that subnational governments could benefit in particular from the implementation of an effective risk management and internal control system which in turn may help to strengthen the local public administration and to reduce the risk of abuse in any economic sector and in a number of areas, including discretionary spending, license and permit administration, and procurement. In fact, these priority areas - risk management and internal control - are also part of the Integrity Model.

Furthermore, the *OECD Recommendation of the Council on Public Integrity* underlines the need to set high standards of conduct for public officials. These clarify which behaviours are expected of public officials and provide a framework for governments to enable ethical behaviour. As emphasised by the OECD Recommendation, it is key to move from a reactive approach that is merely focusing on detecting and sanctioning corrupt individuals (which is necessary, of course), to a proactive approach that seeks to support, to bring together and to makes visible the large majority of public officials that are committed to doing a good job and serving the public interest with integrity.

As such, one of the priorities for regional governments could be to set out standards of conduct and values and clearly communicating the public values and standards to make these alive and part of the organisational culture. These efforts should build on previous experiences and guidance to develop and adopt a code of conduct at local level as described in the "The implementation of the integrity model and function in the regions" sub-section in Chapter 2 (Basel Institute on Governance, 2018[4]), and be led by the SIP with the support of SERVIR and ENAP, especially to mainstream them among senior officials. Other regional governments could follow these examples and develop in a participatory manner a code of conduct that sets out the standards for the public service.

The integrity function within the regional government could lead the participatory process of developing the code and support entities in implementing awareness-raising measures. Such an exercise of developing and implementing a code of conduct is also a good exercise to bring the topic of integrity to the table and can serve as an entry point for a wide variety of other measures and activities (Boehm, 2015[5]). For instance, as a second step, a code of conduct would need to be supported by further guidance, in particular regarding the identification and management of conflict of interest. Furthermore, the integrity function could co-ordinate with Human Resources to develop a specific integrity training in order to train local public officials in public ethics and managing conflicts of interest. Given the high rotation of staff observed at local levels, such trainings should be repeated regularly and be mandatory for all new employees and types of employment contracts. The current development of an Integrity Induction Module by the SIP in collaboration with the ENAP could be particularly helpful to support such efforts.

Taking into account the relevance senior management has on creating a culture of integrity, specific integrity measures could focus in particular on senior management. By setting the highest integrity standards for leadership, an example can be set which will positively influence the broader civil service. Furthermore, awareness-raising and communication efforts on integrity could focus on those areas which were identified as at-risk sectors or functions in the diagnostic.

The integrity function should lead, guide, support and co-ordinate relevant actors for integrity policies within the regional government

As within entities at the national level, the integrity function is not – and should not be – in charge of the implementation of all aspects of the integrity policies in the regional government. In coherence with the tasks and priorities proposed above, it has the key role of articulating and supporting all relevant actors/units within the regional government in view of ensuring an effective implementation of the integrity model, thereby promoting a culture of integrity and strengthening trust of citizens. As a consequence, it cannot resolve the weaknesses of the other areas or units within the regional government.

This role of articulation can be particularly challenging, because of the nascent or absent status of the integrity function within Regional Governments. In addition, the structural limitations of the regional governments may also affect all relevant actors of the local integrity system. Indeed, the interviews highlighted structural weaknesses related to the budget, organisational arrangements and specialisation of staff. At the same, in one region that has not established the integrity function yet, it was lamented that the lack of such an articulation role resulted in poor knowledge of relevant initiatives or tools across the regional government that could support other actors' integrity action without any additional investment.

Building on the analysis of the functions of these actors as well as on the role that the Institutional Integrity Offices could play in public entities at the central level, as analysed in a previous OECD study (OECD, 2019[3]), the integrity function in regional entities should articulate and contribute to the implementation of the various components of the integrity model by performing the roles as summarised in Figure 3.1.

Figure 3.1. Key roles of the integrity function at regional level

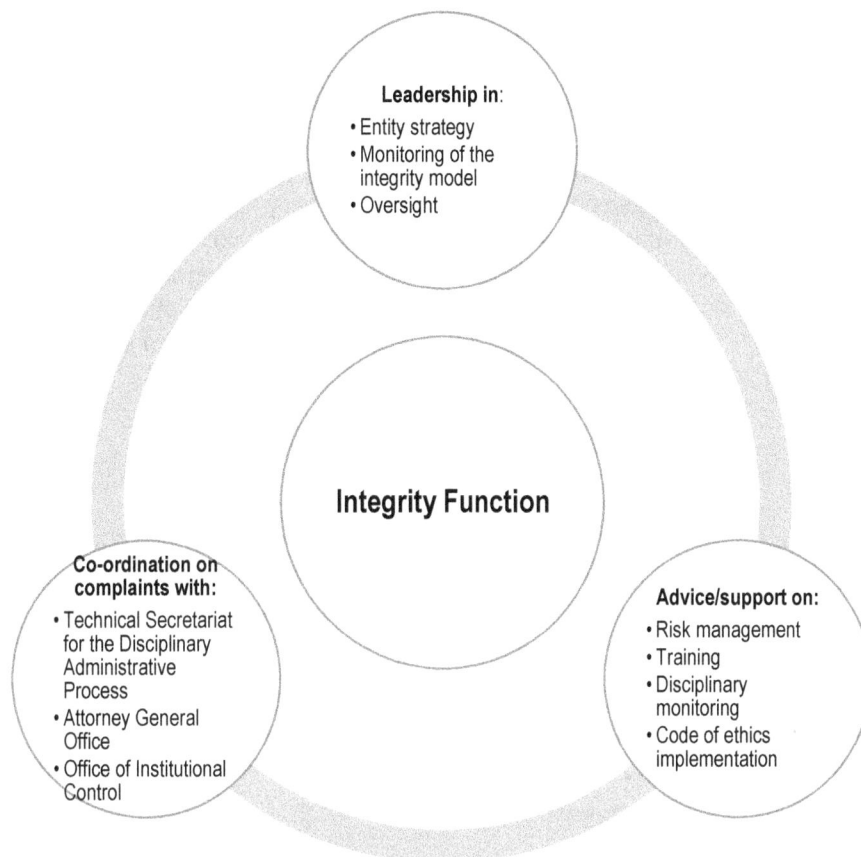

- **Integrity Leadership**: The integrity function shall have and exercise leadership on integrity within the entity, for instance by leading the entity's strategy, monitoring the implementation of the integrity model (e.g. activities, initiatives, sanctions). This requires proactive collaboration from areas responsible for key administrative processes (and risks) such as procurement and budget issues as well as from those directly responsible for all specific elements of the integrity model, such as the Human Resource Office for training activities, the Technical Secretariat for the Disciplinary Administrative Process for disciplinary sanctions, and the Transparency Unit/Person for transparency-related activity. It is also essential that the head of the entity demonstrates support to ensure convening power.

- **Advice and support:** the integrity function shall provide orientation and support to the Governor as well as the units in charge of integrity-related measures such as the Office of Institutional Control for risk identification and oversight of risk mapping, to the Human Resources Office for training activities and monitoring of disciplinary cases, or to the General Secretariat for co-ordinating the implementation of the code of ethics. This task is key for the coherent mainstreaming of all the components of the integrity model in the entity.

- **Co-ordination**: within the complaints' component of the integrity model, the integrity function may be given the role of receiving complaints. If so, the task of the integrity function would consist in transferring them to the relevant actors (e.g. Technical Secretariat for the Disciplinary Administrative Process; Attorney General Office; Office of Institutional Control) and ensure the follow-up, rather than processing them. As highlighted in (OECD, 2019[3]), the processing and investigation of complaints requires substantial resources and would go beyond the preventive role the integrity function is entrusted with in the entity. Co-ordination would also be relevant with the Offices of Institutional Control, dependent on the CGR and part of the external control function.

Indeed, the OCI could verify the implementation of risk management by the regional governments, provide recommendations for improvements and ensure the exchange of information between internal and external control functions, e.g. with respect to integrity risks.

The SIP could scale up both direct and indirect support to the integrity advisory function

The Secretariat for Public Integrity (SIP) plays a key oversight and guidance role on the integrity functions in regional governments because these have to report to it technically and functionally as the leading entity of the National Policy. As part of this mandate defined in Resolution No. 1-2019-PCM/SIP, the SIP can adopt regulations and recommendations of mandatory nature for the integrity functions. In addition, the SIP has been providing assistance to Regional Governments on integrity matters, for example in the framework of the initiative "*La Caravana de la Justicia: Acercando la Justicia a la Ciudadanía*" promoted in 2019 by the Ministry of Justice (Box 3.1).

Box 3.1. SIP integrity support to Regions within the "Caravan of Justice" campaign

In the course of 2019, the Ministry of Justice and Human Rights has promoted the campaign called "The Caravan of Justice: Bringing Justice closer to Citizens", with the aim of bringing all the justice-related services closer to the citizens of all jurisdictions and included an anti-corruption component led by the SIP, which focused on:

- Enabling the creation of OIIs.
- Supporting the Regional Anti-Corruption Commission, including the adoption of the Regional Integrity and Anticorruption Plan.
- Implementing a system of interests declarations.
- Generating capacity on integrity.

This initiative, only concerning five regional governments, allowed the establishment or reactivation of the CRAs in those regions as well as the adoption of the Plan in three of them. At the same time, it allowed to identify some of the reasons behind the little progress in establishing OIIs (the need to modify the ROF, budget considerations, and weak capacity on integrity/anticorruption issues) and implementing interest declarations, which were mostly related to political will and technological gaps.

Source: SIP.

In addition to these efforts, the SIP could further leverage its mandate and strategic role within the CAN to support regions in implementing the integrity function in regional governments. This becomes particularly crucial considering the limited capacity and resources at regional level, but also the need for a strategy to better communicate, clarify and make coherent the understanding and role of public integrity beyond the strict compliance with the law.

Furthermore, the SIP's institutional position within the PCM and the CAN can be further exploited to mobilise political commitment of Governors as well as to facilitate dialogue and co-ordination in those contexts, which could be further enhanced to promote integrity at the regional level (see the "Improved co-ordination at the national level" sub-section in Chapter 3).

For these purposes, the SIP could consider prioritising the following initiatives in both direct and indirect support to the integrity advisory function:

- **Mobilising high-level commitment by making the case for integrity**: interviews during a fact-finding mission and results from a recent survey highlighted that the concept of integrity is often misunderstood and not fully grasped in its potential effects and benefit as a public management tool, both by public officials (Box 2.6) and the Governors. This condition hinders the necessary high-level support and commitment to implement the integrity function but also the integrity model as a whole. The SIP could thus take advantage of events such as the GORE meetings to illustrate the case for integrity, and explain the rationale, objectives and concrete actions to implement the National Policy, the integrity model and the institutionalisation of the integrity function. Such activity could be part of a broader strategy which includes more structured and targeted capacity-building activity recommended for Governors (see the "Raising awareness and building capacities of Governors" sub-section in Chapter 3).

- **Supporting and building capacities of staff working in the regions' integrity function**: regardless of the advancement of the integrity function implementation, interviews during the fact-finding mission and the broader regional context draw the attention to the need for all regions in Peru to create and sustain capacity of the staff working in the integrity function as well as to support them in their efforts. Initiatives in this regard should aim to empower the role of the integrity function within the Regional Government and the region as a whole, but also – and more crucially – to provide guidance, expertise and tools to embrace a priority-based approach to implement the integrity model. In particular, the SIP could promote and follow the process for regions to define the essential tasks to perform based on the matrix but also the corresponding priority components of the integrity model which are to be implemented based on an initial diagnostic. As for capacity building programmes, while those for general staff should be organised and managed at the regional level, eventually with the support of other national entities such as SERVIR, ENAP or the Secretariat for Decentralisation, the SIP could set up a train-the-trainer programme for the head of the integrity function that could be then autonomously replicated internally – possibly in collaboration with local universities and local representatives of association of municipalities – to ensure a minimum coherent set of skills and tasks that they should perform at regional level. These could be carried out in training events by a cluster of regions but also through supporting e-learning material and activities. This could be considered in the current design phase of the capacity-building programme aimed at the integrity function and all incoming public officials – through an Integrity Induction Module – developed by the SIP in collaboration with the ENAP. The SIP could evaluate in how far the integrity function could support the implementation of the integrity training with practical and tailored exercises in the entity.

- **Promoting dialogue between the integrity functions:** Although contexts, including the mandates, for the integrity functions may differ from region to region, a mechanism, e.g. an intranet platform or yearly meetings, could help to ensure coherence, exchange of experiences, tools but also failed attempts which could eventually improve mutual learning and support in the design and implementation of the activities and plans. These mechanisms could also ensure the public recognition of those individuals or entities that championed the promotion of integrity through innovative ideas, as similarly done through the "Integrity Ambassadors" award celebrated during the Integrity Week organised by the SIP (CAN, n.d.[6]).

These activities could take advantage of the expertise built so far. In addition, the SIP already developed some tools and guidance which could be useful for the integrity function, such as the guiding document for developing regional anticorruption plans (CAN, 2015[7]). Furthermore, the SIP could promote synergies with other national initiatives targeting the regions as done for the "Caravan of Justice" (Box 3.1). The enhanced role in support of the regions by the SIP would also require additional resources both in terms of dedicated staff and capacity to convene capacity building or learning-exchange activities.

Strengthening the Regional Anti-corruption Commissions

The limits and challenges that characterise the implementation of the integrity model in Peru's regional governments also reverberate in the broader efforts to establish public integrity systems at regional level, which remains broadly unaccomplished (see the "Regional Anti-corruption Commissions" sub-section in Chapter 2).

As illustrated, Peru decided to create the Regional Anti-corruption Commissions (CRAs), acknowledging the importance of reaching the regions as part of its national policy. Similarly to the role of the CAN at national level, these commissions are meant to articulate initiatives, co-ordinate actions and propose policies to prevent and fight corruption among all relevant stakeholders from public and private sectors in co-ordination and coherence with the broader national efforts. In this way, the CRAs can ultimately ensure the implementation of the National Anti-corruption policy.

Mitigating the underlying weaknesses and establishing key processes for the CRA to fulfil their purpose

While the design of these regional co-ordination mechanisms is potentially capable to address regional issues and risks, the experience has so far demonstrated a limited advance and impact of the CRAs. In fact, not all regional governments have an active CRA or have appointed a Technical Secretariat. In addition, among those CRAs that are active, some have not adopted the internal regulation and many are still missing a plan (Table 2.2 above).

In the cases of those CRAs that have advanced on some elements of assigned functions, interviews suggest that this is mostly dependent on the personal commitment of the members and/or the technical secretary. While the initial outset to create these Commissions is laudable by bringing together the different actors responsible for integrity, reforms are needed to make the CRAs more effective and sustainable without only relying on the political will and support of the heads of the entities comprising the CRAs.

Among the main weaknesses are the lack of institutionalisation of these spaces; the low levels of participation by members, the limitations of the technical secretariats; and the lack of more co-ordinated work with the technical secretariat of the CAN, function now carried out by the SIP (Defensoria del Pueblo, 2018[8]). Interviews with experts and during the fact-finding mission confirmed this situation and highlighted how the key impediments for their success are mainly related to resources and capacity constraints to support the technical work, but also to a lack of focus on priorities and at-risk processes as well as the preponderance of local political dynamics and conflict among the members.

In order to ensure that the CRAs can play the role and have the impact they were set up to do, several elements would need to be reinforced and underlying weaknesses overcome.

First, analysing the outputs and activities of the CRAs, views from experts interviewed confirmed that the CRAs tend to focus on political and legal (enforcement-related) issues, overlooking to assess and address corruption risks and risk sectors throughout the activities and processes of the regional public administration such as the public procurement and budget cycles. To strengthen such a risk-based approach, CRAs could consider involving – either as invitees or permanent members – additional regional actors overseeing key processes and risks such as the decentralised offices of the OSCE or the Regional Development Agencies that are being created. Relevant insights on risks at the municipal level could also be considered by inviting local representatives of municipal associations such as AMPE (*Asociacion De Municipalidades del Perú*) and REMURPE (*Red de Municipalidades Urbanas y Rurales del Perú*). While the participation of additional actors in the CRAs may help bringing additional insights and understanding of such risks, existing members could already take a more risk-based approach to fulfil the envisaged role and tasks, starting with the elaboration of the Regional Anti-corruption Plan.

Second, to support the institutionalisation of the CRAs not only among the public institutions, but also among the population, the standardisation of the organisational structures and operation of the CRAs would be an important step. This would also facilitate the task of the SIP to support the CRAs and allow comparability. The SIP, mandated by the CAN, could develop a model for internal rules of procedures to be adopted which would also address some of the weaknesses currently found. For example, in Colombia the national government developed detailed guidelines for the Regional Moralisation Commissions which include a model for the internal rules of procedures which clearly sets out some of the key aspects, for example, the mission, objectives and functions of the Commission, roles of each member, time period for meetings and progress report. While the CAN has published guidelines for the creation of the CRAs that include key elements for the internal rules of procedure, these are rather vague. This has led to a situation, where, among other aspects, the period in which an ordinary or extraordinary meeting has to be called differs broadly from commission to commission. For example, in the CRA of Ica ordinary meetings have to be held every month, while in Paso no time period is foreseen. In line with the recommendation of the Office of the Ombudsperson, the CAN could consider establishing a reasonable time period in which ordinary meetings have to be held to ensure regularity in the activities of the CRAs, while maintaining a certain level of flexibility. In this way, meetings could also be easier to schedule at, for example, the beginning of the year to ensure availability. This could be included in the internal rules of procedure (Defensoria del Pueblo, 2018[8]).

Third, a factor at times undermining the operation of the CRAs is the commitment and availability of the heads of institutions represented in the CRAs. According to a survey of the Office of the Ombudsperson, in 35% of the CRAs the absence of members in meetings is the principal problem for active work and the cancellation of session because of a lack of quorum (Defensoria del Pueblo, 2018[8]). In line with the recommendation of the Office of the Ombudsperson, in order to facilitate the presence of all institutions at meetings, the internal rules of procedures could include the possibility to nominate an alternative representative. This representative should be of high rank and be given the power to vote in decisions of the CRA. Furthermore, absences without the nomination of a representative should be communicated to the public to build external accountability.

The effectiveness of the CRAs depends not only on the design of the commission and representation of its members in the meetings, but also on their proactive role of its members to contribute to it, provide necessary information, and implement measures and policies agreed within the CRAs. If this is not the case, the CRAs remain another formal body without having little or no impact on entities and, in turn, on citizens. Indeed, the *OECD Recommendation of the Council on Public Integrity* stresses the need to establish responsibilities at all levels not only for designing and leading the integrity system, but also for implementing its elements and policies, including at the organisational level (OECD, 2017[9]). In order to achieve that members of the CRAs actively contribute with proposals and suggestions and to support the implementation of decided initiatives, all members of the CRAs could nominate a technical contact point in their institutions. The contact point would not itself be responsible for any implementation, but rather ensure the continuous support and active participation of the institution in any activity or initiative related to the CRAs, prepare the discussions in the CRAs, provide all necessary information and follow up on commitments undertaken and follow up on any tasks as foreseen in the Regional Anti-corruption plan and report progress for the respective entity. In addition, contact points could create a network to exchange information. The internal rules of procedures could mandate each member of the CRAs to nominate a permanent contact point (Defensoria del Pueblo, 2018[8]).

Fourth, the technical secretary of the CRAs has the role to prepare the meetings of the CRAs, execute the agreements, as well as prepare studies and technical proposals. However, as analysed in the *OECD Integrity Review of Peru* (OECD, 2017[10]), the CRAs technical secretariats are often either inexistent or relatively weak. This was confirmed by a recent analysis of the Ombudsperson Office, in which it found that of the 25 commissions supervised, 17 had a technical secretary (Defensoria del Pueblo, 2018[8]). However, in many cases, they experienced difficulty in fulfiling their functions. These include part-time work, lack of budget to carry out these tasks, and lack of training and specific assistance to enable them to be more efficient in their work (Defensoria del Pueblo, 2018[8]). In many cases, the position of the regional secretary is filled by regional government officials who take on the task on a part-time basis. This affects the eminently technical nature of the secretariats and the need to have specialised personnel experienced in integrity and anti-corruption. As such, it is important to develop and encourage these technical units. Staff from the technical secretariat of the CRAs could receive specific training in Lima, and/or training could be offered at regional levels. Bringing CRAs staff together in Lima would additionally favour cross-regional learning. Also, the technical secretariats would benefit from developing clear internal rules and procedures. Furthermore, the lack of budget for the proper functioning of the technical secretariats has been identified as one of the most important problems facing the commissions in carrying out their activities. The internal rules of procedure of the CRAs could require each member of the CRAs to commit a certain budget to the technical secretary to guarantee operations and build their capacities (OECD, 2017[10]).

Lastly, the support and guidance of the SIP is vital to ensure accountability to the national level and ensure harmonisation throughout the 25 CRAs and with the national level. Since 2017, the SIP actively supports the CRAs through on-site visits and ad-hoc advice. However, to strengthen these efforts, the SIP could implement a virtual platform that allows the exchange and generation of information, both with the SIP and among the CRA. As suggested in the *OECD Integrity Review of Peru* and here, this could provide opportunities for cross-regional learning and policy making in specific areas, for example to improve the design and implementation of regional anti-corruption plans (OECD, 2017[10]).

The integrity function as the transmission belt between the Regional Government, the CRA and the CAN to ensure coherence with the National Policy

Similarly to the proposed approach for the implementation process of the integrity model within regional governments, it is recommended to follow a priority-based incremental approach focused on the essential functions that CRAs are entrusted to perform according to the guidance of the CAN, namely:

- Elaboration of the Regional Anti-corruption Plan.
- To follow up and monitor the implementation and compliance with the National Plan for the Fight against Corruption.
- To report biannually to the CAN on the progress made in the implementation of the Regional Plan for the Fight against Corruption.
- To propose short-, medium- and long-term policies at the regional level for the prevention and fight against corruption (CAN, 2016[11]).

Directive N° 001-2019-PCM/SIP assigns the integrity function the role of the technical secretariat of any commission or other body responsible for integrity and fight against corruption. Furthermore, the guidance provided by the CAN to create CRAs entrusts the Regional Government to provide technical and logistical support needed by the selected entity for the effective performance of its functions (CAN, 2016[11]). In addition to the legal arguments, additional ones can be made to assign the integrity function the role of the technical secretariat of the CRAs:

- The entity in charge of the integrity function in the national government as a whole, which is also the leading entity of the integrity policy at the central level, i.e. the SIP, also performs the role of the technical secretariat for the CAN. This helps to develop a coherent and comprehensive integrity system in Peru.
- The integrity function, which is the only or one of the few bodies with clear mandate to institutionalise integrity at the regional level, could contribute to the same process within the CRAs. Such institutionalisation would be particularly needed to face the reality that very few CRAs have a full-time dedicated Technical Secretariat (Table 2.2), but also to develop regional integrity

systems beyond political dynamics. The latter element is always a reality in all countries and very much so in Peru's regions, and they should not be seen as an impediment, but rather as a strategic factor to be governed through a mature institutional environment consisting of resilient and stable structures (OECD, 2017[10]).

- Further analysing the information on the status of CRAs' implementation, the two regions where the integrity function, through an OII, also perform the technical secretariat of the CRAs, are both among the ones who adopted the internal regulation and regional plan.

In any case, the Regional Governments – through their integrity function – could support the technical secretariat as envisaged by the CAN to: 1) increase their impact; 2) avoid duplication of efforts; and 3) ensure coherence with the National Policy.

In particular, the integrity function could draw on the integrity-related skills, tools and methodologies developed within the regional government and share relevant insights on administrative processes and activities to prioritise the following work of the CRA:

- Based on the risk assessment activity carried out within the GORE, identifying the risk areas and sectors in regions with the input of all other stakeholders, which is the first essential step to develop the regional anticorruption plan and the elaboration of any initiative to be undertaken. Considering the information collected during the fact-finding mission but also the formal mandate and function of the CRAs, risk should be the key guidance criteria of the CRAs' action rather than specific cases under judicial scrutiny.

- Based on these assessments, focus gradually on planned activities, policies and initiatives starting to address issues and sectors emerging as most at risk, leveraging existing work from any of the CRA's members and aiming to produce intermediate results that could be presented to the wider public as evidence of the progress.

- Setting up a reporting system to monitor activities and initiatives related to the National Plan on an annual basis.

- Serve as the transmission belt between the Regional Government, the CRA and the CAN to share good practices, reports on progress but also to request support or ad-hoc assistance that may be needed in terms of knowledge, technical assistance, and political support (Figure 3.2). This role would also provide the opportunity to increase the voice and the active participation of regional governments in national policy making, which has been observed as a key co-ordination challenge in the whole region of Latin America and the Caribbean (OECD, 2019[12]).

Figure 3.2. The role of the integrity function in the regional integrity system

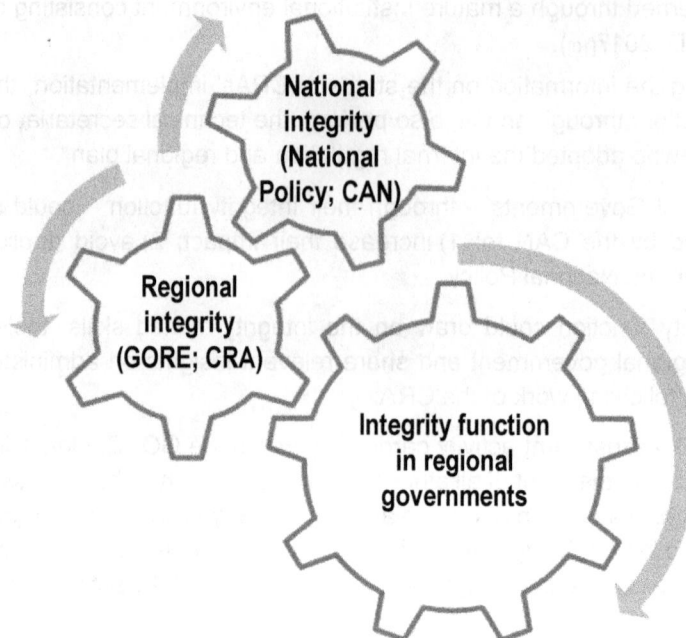

As this role should mostly leverage tasks that the integrity function is already carrying out as part of its work within the entity, this should not create a substantial burden in terms of workload and additional needs. However, the CAN/SIP could consider supporting this role with uniform guidance, material and advice within the broader oversight role over CRAs.

Promoting an enabling environment to integrity from the national level

Raising awareness and building capacities of Governors

As highlighted before, interviews during the fact-finding mission pointed out a low level of awareness among Governors about the essence and relevance of public integrity, as well as its potential as a public management tool. This situation also affects the implementation of the integrity model, whose component no. 1 is 'commitment of senior leadership', and the related required support of Governors to the integrity function in terms of legitimacy, visibility and resources.

In this sense, the SIP could support the mobilisation of high-level commitment by illustrating and making the case for integrity during events such as the Executive GORE. Similarly, the PCM – through the SD and SIP, and the support of the ANGR – could promote the organisation of an annual Integrity GORE (*GORE Integridad*) along the model of Digital GORE (*GORE Digital*), whose first meeting took place in October 2019 in Cajamarca with a session dedicated to integrity.

In addition to these efforts, it is also recommended to provide ad-hoc training to Governors (and possibly the closest advisors) through an induction training at the beginning of the term on public integrity to illustrate the legal elements to be complied with by regional governments, but also – and most importantly – to shape a simple coherent message on the links between integrity and key functions, responsibilities and priorities of the Regional Governments, including on how the entity can benefit from establishing a regional integrity system, and how this can be built progressively based on the capacity, resources and risks of the entity. Such a module could be included in future induction training programmes similar to the ones offered by the Secretariat of Decentralisation for elected mayors in 2018, which are planned to be replicated and eventually institutionalised (Box 3.2).

Box 3.2. Induction programme on Management to Local Authorities in Peru

The Induction programme on Management to Local Authorities consisted in the planning and development of a series of workshops carried out throughout the country between November and December 2018.

The design, organisation and development of the workshops required the co-ordinated mobilisation of a set of actors: officials from the PCM's Decentralisation Secretariat - responsible for the entire programme, the National School of Public Administration - ENAP-SERVIR, in charge of the pedagogical design, who were present in the 25 regions accompanying the working groups, supervising the development of the workshops, supporting the training dynamics and supervising the logistical implementation. Likewise, a University was contracted to develop the training activities of the first day of the Induction programme, providing professors, facilitators and logistics personnel.

Additionally, in response to an announcement from the PCM, officials from 12 ministries, in addition to the General Comptroller of the Republic, the Supervisory Agency of State Contracting (OSCE) and the National Bank went to the regions to facilitate the training spaces on the second day and/or participate in an informative fair. The President of the Republic participated in the opening and/or closing of workshops in 7 regions; the President of the Council of Ministers did so in 6 and in the remaining regions at least one Minister of State participated.

The activity attracted the participation of 1 372 elected mayors from all over the territory. A survey showed their satisfaction and the usefulness of the programme.

The experience of the induction programme represents a pioneering and so far unique effort to bring together local government representatives, put them in dialogue with officials of the State administrative systems, and develop training processes. The rich experience generated, translated into lessons learned, will allow its replication and, eventually, institutionalisation.

Source: GIZ Evaluation Report.

In this context, Peru could also consider the mandatory training programme organised for elected Governors and Mayors in Colombia to promote the co-ordination of the government plans of the incoming local administrations with the National Government and the National Development Plan. This programme is also supported by a Virtual Advisory Space –EVA (*Espacio Virtual de Asesoría*), where public servants, including Governors and Mayors, can request information and receive guidance on the different policies promoted by the entity.

Box 3.3. Induction seminars for elected Governors and Mayors in Colombia

The National School of Public Administration of Colombia (*Escuela Superior de Administración Pública*, ESAP), a public university institution in Colombia, organises and conducts public administration induction seminars for elected Governors and Mayors. Every four years during a week, prior to their possession, all Governors and Mayors of the country meet in Bogotá to receive guidance on various issues of public administration. Attendance at these seminars is mandatory and is one of the requirements to take office (Article 31 of Law 489 of 1998).

Representatives of various national Government institutions also participate in this space to directly provide training on topics such as strategic planning, efficient purchasing, financial management, international co-operation, among others. In the most recent version of the seminar, the President of Colombia, the Post-Conflict Minister, the High Commissioner for Peace, among others, participated delivering talks on strategic issues for the country. In addition to these general talks, Governors and Mayors participate in specific workshops for their regions and municipalities.

These seminars are part of the strategy called '*Elijo saber: Candidatos formados, gobiernos exitosos*', led by the ESAP, the National Planning Department, and the Administrative Department of Public Service -FP, with the support of several entities including the Attorney General's Office, the Ministry of Information Technology and Telecommunications and the National Electoral Council. Within the framework of this strategy, candidates for mayor and governor receive virtual and face-to-face training in topics related to electoral political regime, territorial development management and local public management.

In addition, as part of the activities promoted by the National Government to support territorial development management, FP has a Virtual Advisory Space –EVA (*Espacio Virtual de Asesoría*), where public servants, including Governors and Mayors, can request information and receive guidance on the different policies promoted by the entity, including public employment, citizen participation and transparency, organisational structure, among others.

Source: Departamento Administrativo de la Función Pública (2015), En Bogotá avanza capacitación a Gobernadores y Alcaldes electos de todo el país en el marco de la estrategia Elijo Saber, https://www.funcionpublica.gov.co/web/guest/noticias/-/asset_publisher/mQXU1au9B4LL/content/en-bogota-avanza-capacitacion-a-gobernadores-y-alcaldes-electos-de-todo-el-pais-en-el-marco-de-la-estrategia-elijo-saber?from=2017/04; Federación Colombiana de Municipios (2015), A través de la estrategia elijo saber se capacitará a ciudadanos de todo el país, https://www.fcm.org.co/?p=2984, accessed September 2019.

Lastly, efforts should continue in monitoring the ethical climate among public officials at the regional level as recently done by SERVIR since the evolution of the results over time provides a valuable indication of high-level commitment together with a broader understanding of gaps and challenges in establishing a culture of integrity in regional entities, including the perception that senior managers do not abide by the conflict of interest policy (Box 2.6).

Improved co-ordination at the national level

Considering Peru's decentralised administrative model and the resulting influence of several national actors on regional governments and their integrity systems), nationally co-ordinated mechanisms can provide additional complementary support to the integrity function and ecosystem at the regional level. In doing so, these mechanisms could ensure avoiding gaps and overlaps between initiatives of different actors, thereby guaranteeing greater efficiency and impact.

Through the CAN

The High-level Commission against Corruption (*Comisión Alto-nivel de Anti-corrupción*, CAN) is Peru's anticorruption co-ordination mechanism that was established by Law no. 29976 and its regulation in decree no. 089-2013-PCM, which also outlines CAN's mandate and responsibilities. The CAN is formed by public and private institutions and civil society, and co-ordinates efforts and actions on anti-corruption cross institutions and levels of government. It includes, among members, the president of the National Assembly of Regional Governments, and its responsibilities include supporting the implementation of the CRAs, and co-ordinating with them the implementation of the National Policy and Plan.

In order to improve the fulfilment of such responsibilities towards regions, the CAN could consider a number of priorities which draw from the assessment of the *OECD Integrity Review of Peru* (OECD, 2017[10]) and the challenges identified in the "Strenghtening the Regional Anti-corruption Commissions" section in Chapter 3. In implementing these initiatives, given the pivotal role envisaged for the integrity function in the broader regional perspective, but also SIP's role within the CAN, they should be coherently and complementarily developed with SIP's support activity to regions' integrity functions. These are:

- The CAN could strengthen the capacities of the technical secretariats of the CRAs through a focused capacity development strategy. Staff from the technical secretariat of the CRAs could receive specific training in Lima, with additional sessions to be organised at macro-regional levels to address local challenges. These activities should focus on operational aspects of the CRA's functioning, including risk assessment, prioritisation, planning, and internal procedures. Depending on the area or aspect to be addressed, these activities would be co-ordinated by the SIP with input from various members of the CAN depending on the topic or area.

- To ensure coherence and knowledge transfer between the national and the regional levels, an effective co-ordination mechanism leveraging IT tools and platforms between the CAN and the CRAs could be institutionalised. As previously illustrated, the integrity function could play a greater role as the integrity transmission belt between the national and regional levels, including within the CAN (see "Strengthening the Regional Anti-corruption Commissions" sub-section in Chapter 3). On top of this, the CAN could further develop IT initiatives such as the web-based platform to submit information on progress or public integrity indicators to enable public monitoring and benchmarking which are being developed but have not yet been implemented.

- A mechanism could help to ensure information and experience sharing between regions in order to improve mutual learning – especially among regions with similar economic context – on risks, achievements and priority issues, e.g. starting with the design and implementation of the regional anti-corruption plans. On the one hand, this could be part of the intranet platform being implemented by the CAN; on the other hand, dedicated sessions for mutual learning could be included in the capacity-building events proposed above. Content-wise, these mechanisms should focus on common priorities and challenges but also trans-regional issues that can only be tackled through enhanced co-operation. Similarly to the proposal made for integrity functions, in order to incentivise the active participation of CRAs, this mechanism could also provide rewards in the form of public recognition or awards to "champion CRAs" bringing success stories and model that could be replicated in other regional context.

Within the executive through the PCM

The Presidency of the Council of Ministers (PCM), the government's main centre-of-government institution reporting to the head of government and serving the head of government and Cabinet, could also promote co-ordination efforts in support of regional integrity systems. As illustrated, many of the most relevant actors of Peru's public integrity system – starting with SIP, but also SERVIR and SGP – are part of the PCM. Furthermore, the PCM also includes the Secretariat for Decentralisation, whose mission is to ensure a coherent and consistent decentralisation process. As such, it is essential that all these authorities (*entes rectores*) co-ordinate to ensure that the guidance and directives issued in their respective policy domains are coherent, do not create overlapping or duplicating efforts, and do not send mixed messages.

Given that PCM is also in charge of co-ordinating multi-sectoral policies and programmes within the executive, it could also play a role in promoting co-ordination between actors with direct influence on integrity policies and those leading entities in key risk integrity areas such as public procurement . In particular, it could propose the establishment of an inter-ministerial working group focused on developing tools and methodologies to support the identification and mitigation of integrity risks in procurement processes at regional level, which experts consider not been sufficiently addressed in regional integrity strategies (e.g. in the context of the CAN). Such group could include representatives from the Ministry of Finance (OSCE and Peru Compra) together with PCM's entities such as the SIP and Secretariat for Decentralisation. Indeed, inter-ministerial working groups can be created in Peru for setting courses of action that will contribute to the proper implementation of multi-sector public policies (OECD, 2016[13]). At the same time, the group could build on the OSCE's recent report on 'Assessment and Strategy for Risk-management in Public Procurement' (*'Diagnóstico y Estrategia para la Gestión de Riesgos en Contratación Pública'*), which identifies 81 risks affecting the efficiency, competition as well as the integrity of the public procurement cycle (Organismo Supervisor de las Contrataciones del Estado, OSCE, 2020[14]).

Through the Regional Development Agencies

A key initiative co-ordinated by the PCM that could both support and benefit from regional integrity systems are the Regional Development Agencies (RDAs). RDA's are mechanisms for the cross-sector and intergovernmental co-ordination of a territory's specific priorities, involving public and private actors (i.e. all levels of government, private enterprise, academia, and civil society).

The establishment of the RDAs is a major opportunity to support goals promoted by the decentralisation process and thus to bring benefits to citizens and the country as a whole. However, it also entails various integrity risks linked to the fact that the RDAs will be responsible for deciding priorities and channelling considerable amounts of public funds. On the one hand, the RDAs' central role in regional decision making and administrative processes will enable them to oversee the management of regional resources and thus to oversee and understand risk areas and activities, so they could provide useful insights to the CRAs, especially in their risk mapping and assessment activities. Depending on the RDAs' legal status and composition, CRAs could even consider inviting them to meetings or to have them joining as members. On the other hand, it is essential that RDAs have adequate mechanisms and processes in place to avoid undue influence (policy capture).

For example, the on-going process to establish priorities and areas for RDAs requires technical input in the form of studies and consultancies that will have great weight in the assessment. However, interviews during the fact-finding mission highlighted that in some cases the people or entities capable of providing these services at the regional level are limited in numbers and often linked to – if not financed by – those participating in the commissions that are entrusted to make decisions concerning the RDA's planning. These dynamics require designing and establishing RDAs with necessary integrity safeguards that could naturally leverage the regional integrity infrastructure and policies, and are in line with the OECD strategy to preventing policy capture and promoting integrity in public decision making (Figure 3.3).

Figure 3.3. The OECD strategy to prevent policy capture and promote integrity in public decision making

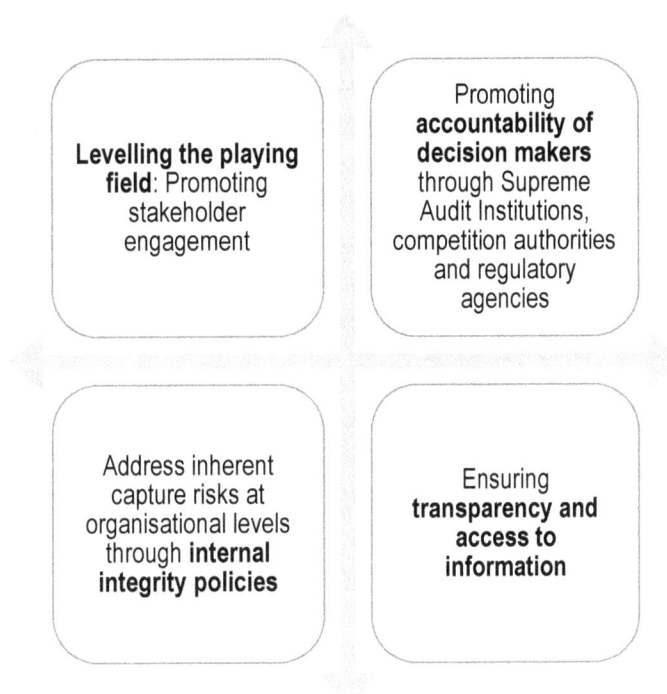

Source: (OECD, 2017[15]).

For this purpose, the need for support from the PCM is twofold:

- First, to mainstream integrity in the RDAs by entrusting the integrity function of the Regional Government to provide them with advice in articulating and co-ordinating relevant integrity initiatives. Therefore, the PCM could mobilise relevant actors at both national and regional level – including Governors – to support and promote the added-value of establishing an integrity function in Regional Governments as well as to discuss and define the most appropriate role and responsibilities within the RDAs.

- Second, to define minimum internal integrity policies addressing the inherent risks of capture of the RDAs, e.g. a conflict-of-interest disclosure policy for those making key decisions.

Given that the implementation of the RDAs is taking place in sequence across regions, this twofold intervention could be first piloted in a few regions where the level of maturity of the RDAs is more advanced and where advice on integrity would be thus most needed.

Through the Inter-ministerial Working Group

The temporary Inter-ministerial Working Group was created in 2019 with a 4-month mandate to improve organisational and human resources management in regional governments. In this way, the Working Group responded to the challenges experienced by subnational entities – also corroborated during the fact-finding mission – to establish organisational structures that respond to their necessities and capacities, as well as in implementing regulation and updating management tools.

The Working Group adopted an action plan envisaging the development of a total of nine documents, tools and programmes to standardise, guide and build capacity on organisational management and human resources in subnational entities. In addition, the working group engaged bilaterally with some regional entities, for example by supporting the regional government of Ucayali in the update of its Organisational and Functions Regulation (*Reglamento de Organización y Funciones*, ROF).

This Working Group addressed key structural challenges of Peru's regions; however, integrity was not among the key dimension being considered. In the future, it would be beneficial for similar working groups to include the SIP and consider integrity as a cross-cutting value and tool for public management and co-ordinate with other national initiatives to build on existing efforts and amplify the impact of its work.

Regional monitoring and benchmarking to incentivise integrity efforts

An additional way to promote and create incentives for implementing integrity systems at the regional level is to monitor and benchmark their "integrity" performance through indices related to issues such as the implementation of the integrity function (for the government) and the CRA (for the regions as a whole).

Although *strictu-sensu* indices are measurement tools, the ways that integrity-related indices are conceived are relevant for the definition of minimum standards or elements that are expected to be present in the integrity systems of public institutions, including subnational governments. They also introduce a competitive factor and offer possibilities of visibility for both achievement and failure. Some of these indices are made by national governments or control institutions (Korea, Colombia, Spain or Austria) or by civil society organisations (TI-Colombia, or the European Transparency Index for Cities developed by TI-Slovakia), or both. While the impact of these indexes is not unequivocal, there are indications that those indices create a "pull-factor" for local governments who want to claim credit for reform, or at least make it visible.

For this to be effective, monitoring should be carried out in a public and transparent manner, for instance through scorecards or indices. Both the SIP (for regional governments) and the CAN (for CRAs) could consider a similar approach as a means of communicating progress to citizens more easily, and applying political and social pressure to implement reforms.

Box 3.4. Monitoring performance of Anti-corruption Commission in Colombia

The Anti-corruption Observatory in Colombia has developed composite indices on topics such as fiscal performance and open government, which are available by region and municipality. This allows the public to benchmark and compare. One index measures the progress of regional anti-corruption systems (*Comisiones Regionales de Morazalización*) and assesses their compliance with legislation, including: number of meetings/consultations with citizens, quality of action plans, and implementation of action plan items.

The Figure below shows the ranking results according to these indicators. Results are available in numerical and map form, whereby regions are colour coded according to their scores. Regions in red and yellow are behind those coloured in green.

Figure 3.4. Ranking visualisation

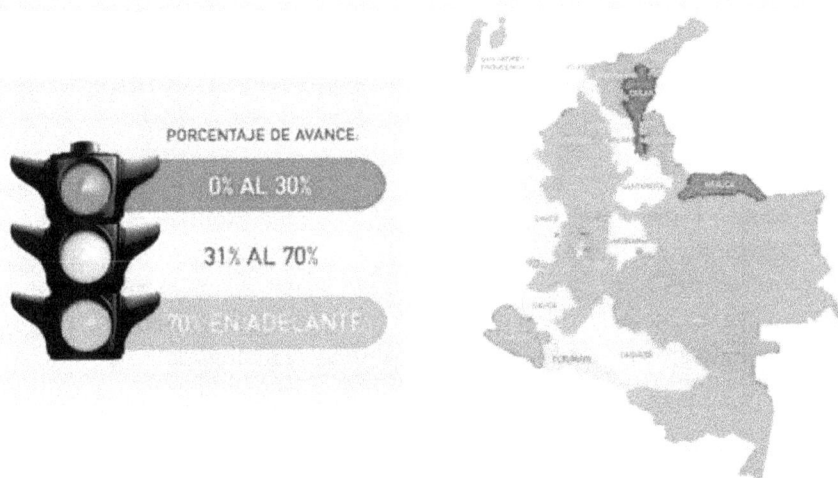

Source: (OECD, 2017[16]).

Whole-of-society communication and awareness raising to enable citizens and the private sector to demand action from government

One of the value-added of the CAN and CRAs' model is that it brings together several institutions from the public and private sectors and civil society to promote co-ordination and improve the integrity system across the country. However, interviews during fact-finding mission showed that societal actors are relatively unaware of the efforts and initiatives being taken to implement local integrity systems at regional level.

This factor also hinders the full potential of public integrity, which is not just an issue for the public sector: individuals, civil society and companies shape interactions in society and their actions can harm or foster integrity in their communities. This is also asserted by the *OECD Recommendation of the Council on Public Integrity* that promotes a whole-of-society approach to integrity: since all these actors interact with public officials and play a critical role in setting the public agenda and influencing public decisions, they also have a responsibility to promote public integrity. Awareness-raising efforts, education and consultation mechanisms are three essential features to communicate standards externally that Peruvian institutions could consider putting in place at both central and regional level to target local groups of individuals, civil society and companies. In this sense, an initiative was organised by the SIP in 2019 - the Integrity Week (*Semana de la Integridad*) - which offered various typologies of open events (e.g. panels, presentations, awarding ceremony, hackathons, movies, etc.). Some of these were organised outside of Lima. These events aimed to reflect on the effects of corruption and how citizens and other stakeholders can contribute to raising the standards of public integrity through active participation and mutual recognition (Presidencia del Consejo de Ministros, PCM, n.d.[17]). Based on the results of these events, the SIP could develop a communication strategy to reach citizens at all levels of government. This strategy could foresee different communication channels and events, involve key stakeholders from the government, private sector and civil society, and be part of a longer-term strategy to strengthen integrity.

At the same time, CRAs – in close collaboration with local universities and active actors from civil society – could promote on-line training courses on the social benefits of issues related to public integrity such as the culture of legality and civic responsibilities (Box 3.5). Any stakeholder having a relationship or interaction with the public sector could even be encouraged to enroll and take part in this e-learning course by offering incentives for completion, such as issuing a certificate identifying them as "Citizen for Integrity" or "Business for Integrity" (OECD, 2018[18]).

Box 3.5. Interactive training to promote a culture of legality: Nuevo León's government, civil society and private sector initiative

The "Let's Do It Right!" Initiative has launched an interactive online training course on the culture of legality. The website also provides free access to tools to help citizens of Nuevo León recognise the social benefits of supporting the rule of law in their communities in order to transform their cities. The online training is provided free of charge. The course offers an introduction to the principles of a culture of legality, an explanation of the importance of a culture of legality and the role of citizens. It describes the barriers to and mechanisms for creating a culture of legality in their communities.

The course also provides citizens with basic information on principles of the rule of law and the role of citizens in respecting the rule of law and changing their interactions in society. After completing the course, participants take an examination, and on passing, receive a certificate of completion.

Source: (OECD, 2018[18]).

References

Basel Institute on Governance (2018), *Guía para la implementación participativa de un Código de Conducta*, http://gfpsubnacional.pe/wp-content/uploads/2018/12/Forteleciendo-la-Gesti%C3%B3n-Descentraliza_final.pdf. [4]

Boehm, F. (2015), "Códigos de comportamiento para la administración pública", *Revista Digital de Derecho Administrativo*, Vol. 14, pp. 65-89. [5]

CAN (2016), *Lineamientos para la creación de Comisiones Regionales Anticorrupción*, Comisión de Alto Nivel Anticorrupción, https://can.pcm.gob.pe/wp-content/uploads/2016/07/Lineamientos-creaci%c3%b3n-de-Comisiones-Regionales-Anticorrupci%c3%b3n.pdf. [11]

CAN (2015), *Guía para la formulación de planes regionales anticorrupción pasos y cronograma*, Comisión de Alto Nivel Anticorrupción, https://can.pcm.gob.pe/wp-content/uploads/2015/08/GUIA-PARA-LA-FORMULACION-DE-PLANES-REGIONALES-ANTICORRUPCION.pdf. [7]

CAN (n.d.), *Concurso Nacional Embajadores de la Integridad 2019*, Comisión de Alto Nivel Anticorrupción, https://can.pcm.gob.pe/embajadores2019/ (accessed on 28 May 2020). [6]

Defensoria del Pueblo (2018), "Comisiones Regionales Anticorrupción: Diagnóstico y recomendaciones para mejorar su funcionamiento", *Boletín: Supervisión de Espacios Anticorrupción, Diciembre 2018 - Año I - №2*, https://www.defensoria.gob.pe/wp-content/uploads/2018/12/BOLETIN-ANTICURRUPCION.pdf (accessed on 12 June 2020). [8]

Instituto Nacional de Estadística e Informática (2020), *Perú: Percepción ciudadana sobre gobernabilidad, democracia y confianza en las instituciones*, http://m.inei.gob.pe/media/MenuRecursivo/boletines/informe_de_gobernabilidad_may2020.pdf (accessed on 6 November 2020). [2]

OECD (2019), *La Integridad Pública en América Latina y el Caribe 2018-2019: De Gobiernos reactivos a Estados proactivos*, OECD, Paris, http://www.oecd.org/gov/integridad/integridad-publica-en-america-latina-caribe-2018-2019.htm (accessed on 25 February 2020). [12]

OECD (2019), *Offices of Institutional Integrity in Peru: Implementing the Integrity System*, OECD, Paris, http://www.oecd.org/gov/ethics/offices-of-institutional-integrity-peru.pdf. [3]

OECD (2018), *OECD Integrity Review of Nuevo León, Mexico: Sustaining Integrity Reforms*, OECD Public Governance Reviews, OECD Publishing, Paris, https://dx.doi.org/10.1787/9789264284463-en. [18]

OECD (2017), *OECD Integrity Review of Mexico: Taking a Stronger Stance Against Corruption*, OECD Public Governance Reviews, OECD Publishing, Paris, https://dx.doi.org/10.1787/9789264273207-en. [16]

OECD (2017), *OECD Integrity Review of Peru: Enhancing Public Sector Integrity for Inclusive Growth*, OECD Public Governance Reviews, OECD Publishing, Paris, https://dx.doi.org/10.1787/9789264271029-en. [10]

OECD (2017), *OECD Recommendation of the Council on Public Integrity*, OECD/LEGAL/0435, https://legalinstruments.oecd.org/en/instruments/OECD-LEGAL-0435. [9]

OECD (2017), *Preventing Policy Capture: Integrity in Public Decision Making*, OECD Public Governance Reviews, OECD Publishing, Paris, https://dx.doi.org/10.1787/9789264065239-en. [15]

OECD (2016), *OECD Public Governance Reviews: Peru: Integrated Governance for Inclusive Growth*, OECD Public Governance Reviews, OECD Publishing, Paris, https://dx.doi.org/10.1787/9789264265172-en. [13]

Organismo Supervisor de las Contrataciones del Estado, OSCE (2020), *Diagnóstico y Estrategia para la Gestión de Riesgos en Contratación Pública*, https://cdn.www.gob.pe/uploads/document/file/1038474/Diagn%C3%B3stico_y_Estrategia_para_la_Gestion_de_Riesgos_en_Contrataci%C3%B3n_P%C3%BAblica.pdf (accessed on 29 September 2020). [14]

Presidencia del Consejo de Ministros, PCM (n.d.), *Semana de la Integridad 2019*, https://www.gob.pe/institucion/pcm/campa%C3%B1as/578-semana-de-la-integridad-2019 (accessed on 5 May 2020). [17]

Shack, Pérez and Portugal (2020), "Cálculo del tamaño de la corrupción y la inconducta funcional en el Perú: Una aproximación exploratoria. Documento de Política en Control Gubernamental", Contraloría General de la República, Lima, Perú, https://doc.contraloria.gob.pe/estudios-especiales/documento_trabajo/2020/Calculo_de_la_Corrupcion_en_el_Peru.pdf (accessed on 6 November 2020). [1]

4 Proposals for action to implement integrity systems in the Peruvian regions

This Chapter provides an overview of the actions proposed in the report to implement integrity systems at the regional level in Peru. The overview is organised in two tables. One table includes the recommendations aimed at enhancing integrity in regional governments, in particular through the integrity function. The second table reports the recommendations related to the strengthening of the Regional Anticorruption Commissions. For each recommendation, the tables clarify the responsible actors(s) and, when relevant, those with whom co-ordination should be established.

The *OECD Recommendation of the Council on Public Integrity* (OECD, 2017[1]) underlines the need to establish a risk-based integrity system at all levels of government to strengthen integrity and prevent corruption effectively. While co-ordination is key, it is also vital that the integrity system reflects specific integrity challenges and opportunities. In principle, the creation of the CRAs and the establishment of the integrity function in the regional government have the potential to address corruption risks and integrity challenges at the regional level in co-ordination with the national level, However, further efforts are necessary to strengthen the CRAs and institutionalise the integrity function to ultimately effectively promote integrity and fight corruption at the regional level.

Table 4.1. Overview of the key recommendations respective to the integrity function and integrity in the regional government more broadly

Recommendation	Actor in charge
Strengthening a strategic approach to integrity based on evidence, the regional governments, in co-ordination with the SIP, could: 1. identify priorities based on a diagnostic tool assessing the internal strengths and weaknesses and external opportunities and threats of the regional government (also known as SWOT-analysis); and 2. build on the diagnostic, select the priorities for strengthening integrity, determine the entity or unit responsible for defining a plan to implement such priorities and develop indicators to monitor advances in that area.	Regional governments in collaboration with SIP
Responding to the specific challenges and opportunities in every region, an incremental approach for the integrity function could be developed. Regions would be categorised according to: • size, which may also serve as proxy for the level of institutional capacities, available resources and support needed • exogenous or environmental integrity risk levels and typologies of each region. The tasks fulfiled by the integrity function should as a minimum be related to risk assessment, integrity policy and monitoring of the integrity model's implementation.	SIP (developing incremental approach in co-ordination with regional governments)

To mainstream integrity effectively, the integrity function in regional governments should articulate and contribute to the implementation of the various components of the integrity model by performing the roles of:
• Leadership in:
  - Entity strategy
  - Monitoring of the integrity model
  - Oversight
• Advice/support on:
  - Risk management
  - Training
  - Disciplinary monitoring
  - Code of ethics implementation
• Co-ordinating on complaints with
  - Technical Secretariat for the Disciplinary Administrative Process
  - Attorney General Office
  - Office of Institutional Control
	Integrity function in regional governments

Supporting the integrity function, the SIP could scale up both direct and indirect support, through: • Mobilising high-level commitment by making the case for integrity; e.g. during events such as the Executive GORE. Similarly, the PCM – through the SD and SIP, and the support of the ANGR – could promote the organisation of an annual Integrity GORE (GORE Integridad) along the model of Digital GORE (GORE Digital). • Supporting and building capacities of staff working in the regions' integrity function, through training events by cluster of regions, in addition to e-learning material and activities. • Promoting dialogue between the integrity functions via an intranet platform or yearly meetings, to ensure coherence, exchange of experiences, mutual learning and support in the design and implementation of the activities and plans.	SIP
Creating awareness among regional governments, the SIP could provide ad-hoc training to Governors (and possibly the closest advisors) through an induction training at the beginning of the term on public integrity.	SIP in co-ordination with Secretariat of Decentralisation
Providing valuable evidence on integrity, efforts should continue in monitoring the ethical climate among public officials at the regional level.	SERVIR in co-ordination with SIP
Ensuring coherence and knowledge transfer between the national and the regional levels, an effective co-ordination mechanism leveraging IT tools and platforms between the CAN and the regional level, namely the CRAs and integrity function could be institutionalised. This could also include a web-based platform to submit information on progress or public integrity indicators to enable a public monitoring and benchmarking.	CAN

The PCM could lead efforts to promote co-ordination on integrity among actors in the executive with direct influence on integrity policies and those leading entities in key risk integrity areas such as public procurement. It could propose the establishment of an inter-ministerial working group focused on developing tools and methodologies to support the identification and mitigation of integrity risks in procurement processes at regional level. Such group could include representatives from Ministry of Finance (OSCE and Peru Compra) together with PCM's entities such as the SIP and Secretariat for Decentralisation. At the same time, the group could build on the OSCE's recent report on 'Assessment and Strategy for Risk-management in Public Procurement' ('Diagnóstico y Estrategia para la Gestión de Riesgos en Contratación Pública'), which identifies 81 risks affecting the efficiency, competition as well as integrity of the public procurement cycle.	PCM, in collaboration with OSCE and Peru Compra
Promoting integrity in the RDAs, the PCM could pilot the following approach: 1. Entrusting the integrity function of the Regional Government to provide the RDAs with advice in articulating and co-ordinating relevant integrity initiatives. 2. Defining minimum internal integrity policies addressing the inherent risks of capture of the RDAs, e.g. a conflict-of-interest disclosure policy for those taking key decisions.	PCM in collaboration with regional governments
Promoting and creating incentives for the implementation of integrity systems at the regional level, the SIP could develop a regional monitoring and benchmarking for the regional governments´ "integrity" performance through indices related to issues such as the implementation of the integrity function (for the government) and of the CRA (for the regions as a whole). In this way, progress could also be communicated to citizens and political and social pressure created to implement reforms in case of regions lagging behind.	SIP

Table 4.2. Overview of the recommendations respective to the CRAs

Recommendation	Actor in charge
Strengthening the adoption of a risk-based approach, CRAs could consider involving – either as invitees or permanent members – additional regional actors overseeing key processes and risks such as the decentralised offices of the OSCE or the Regional Development Agencies. In addition, relevant insights on risks at the municipal level could also be considered by inviting local representatives of municipal associations such as AMPE (Asociacion De Municipalidades del Perú) and REMURPE (Red de Municipalidades Urbanas y Rurales del Perú).	CRAs
Supporting the institutionalisation of the CRAs not only among the public institutions, but also among the population, the organisational structures and operation of the CRAs could be standardised. The SIP, in line with its function to provide technical support to the High-level Commission against Corruption (CAN), could develop a model for internal rules of procedures to be adopted. Furthermore, the CAN could consider establishing a reasonable time period in which ordinary meetings have to be held to ensure regularity in the activities of the CRAs.	SIP and CAN
Facilitating the presence of all institutions at meetings, the internal rules of procedures could include the possibility to nominate an alternative representative. This representative should be of high rank and be given the power to vote in decisions of the CRA. Furthermore, absences without the nomination of a representative should be communicated to the public to build external accountability.	SIP and CRAs
The internal rules of procedures could mandate each member of the CRA to nominate a permanent contact point to engage members of the CRA to contribute actively with proposals and suggestions. The contact point would be responsible for preparing the discussions in the CRA, providing all necessary information, follow up on commitments undertaken and on any tasks as foreseen in the Regional Anti-corruption plan, and report progress for the respective entity. In addition, contact points could create a network to exchange information.	SIP
Building capacities, the SIP could train staff from the technical secretariat of the CRAs. Efforts could be supported by the members of the CAN. These training activities should focus on operational aspects of the CRA's functioning, including risk assessment, prioritisation, planning, and internal procedures.	SIP (in collaboration with members of CAN)
Providing the CRAs with adequate financial resources, the internal rules of procedure of the CRAs could require each member of the CRAs to commit a certain budget to the technical secretary to guarantee operations and build their capacities	SIP in co-ordination with CRAs
Allowing for the exchange and generation of information, the SIP could implement a virtual platform for the CRAs. This could provide opportunities for cross-regional learning and policy making in specific areas, for example, to improve the design and implementation of regional anti-corruption plans.	SIP
The Integrity function could assume the role of technical secretary of the CRAs ensuring co-ordination between the CRA and the regional government.	CRAs
Raising awareness of integrity and the mandate of the CRAs, the CRAs, in close collaboration with local universities and active actors from civil society, could promote on-line training courses on the social benefits of issues related to public integrity such as the culture of legality and civic responsibilities.	CRAs
Promoting and creating incentives for the implementation of integrity systems at the regional level, the CAN could develop an index measuring the performance of the CRAs. In this way, progress could also be communicated to citizens and political and social pressure created to implement reforms in case of regions lagging behind.	CAN

References

OECD (2017), *OECD Recommendation of the Council on Public Integrity*, OECD/LEGAL/0435, [1]
https://legalinstruments.oecd.org/en/instruments/OECD-LEGAL-0435.

Annex A. Existing integrity functions at the regional level in Peru

Table A A.1. Status of implementation of the integrity function at the regional level and its features

	Implementing body	Instrument to implement the integrity function	Functions assigned by the implementing instruments
Amazonas	Human Resources Department	Regional Resolution (2019)	• Receive complaints about corruption allegations and containing request for whistleblowing protection. • Assess facts and document supporting allegations and adopt protection measures to whistleblower or witness. • Assess whether the complaint is in bad faith and take consequent measures. • Transfer the complaint and supporting documents to the Technical Secretariat for disciplinary proceedings or the Public Attorney. • Co-ordinate the capacity building activities with the Human Resources Department. • Lead, participate and follow up the process to adopt the GORE's anti-corruption plan.
Cajamarca	Permanent task force in the General Regional Management department consisting of: • Regional General Manager • Human Resources Department • General Secretary • Advisor to the Regional General Management	Regional Resolution (2020)	Those of Resolution No. 1-2019-PCM/SIP.
La Libertad	Functional unit in the General Regional Management department	Regional Resolution (2018)	• Co-ordinate actions between the CRA and the regional institutions' anti-corruption units. • Formulate, propose, implement and monitor anti-corruption mechanisms, regulations and guidelines in the Regional Government, as well as develop actions on transparency, access to improve information, ethics and institutional integrity. • Participate in the formulation, implementation and evaluation of the Regional Government anti-corruption plan. • Receive and process complaints from public officials of the Regional Government or third parties, ensuring the confidentiality of the information. • Assess and verify the truth of the acts underlying the complaints. • Promote mechanisms and administrative incentives allowing for an ethical and transparent organisational culture. • Promote awareness-raising activities in co-ordination with the General Regional Management department and the Human Resources sub-department.

Implementing body	Instrument to implement the integrity function	Functions assigned by the implementing instruments
		• Propose and define administrative incentives to those that detect and report any act of corruption. • Transfer the reports on corruption to the relevant authorities in charge of administrative or criminal responsibility. • Co-ordinate the preparation of public hearings to present anticorruption actions. • Manage and maintain the Transparency Portal. • Other functions, given by regulation, or assigned by the regional government.
Lambayeque	Institutional Integrity Regional Office	Modification to Organisation and Functions Regulation	• Promote ethics in public service and propose tools to address corruption risks in regional public management. • Design and propose policies and procedures to improve public financial management. • Propose mechanisms and technical-regulatory documents for the entity, in order to ensure the implementation of national standards issued within the framework of the functional integrity and anti-corruption system. • Develop integrity and anti-corruption indicators to enable the monitoring and adoption of public policies. • Design, conduct the process leading to the approval, and follow up on the compliance with the regional integrity plan and the fight against corruption in regional public management. • To prepare periodic reports on compliance, the quality and accessibility of public information contained on the websites, and the standard transparency portal, of the different agencies with regard to the obligations imposed by the law in the area of transparency. • To receive and guide the correct processing of any complaint filed by a natural or legal person, with respect to alleged irregular acts or failure to perform duties by the employee or officer of the entity. • To participate in the organisation and activities of the regional anti-corruption commission of Lambayeque, constituting the technical secretariat of this consultation space. • Promote the creation and operation of an internal system to combat corruption in the regional public administration. • Promote and co-ordinate with the executive office of human resources of the entity, the training of personnel in matters related to probity in the exercise of public service and the application of values and transparency that guarantee a better service to citizens. • Promote a culture of integrity, at the regional level, through public sector bodies, the private sector, universities, the media and civil society. • Other functions, given by regulation, or assigned by the regional government.
Piura	Functional unit in the Presidency of the Regional Council, reporting to the Anticorruption Technical Secretariat	Modification to Organisation and Functions Regulation (2011)	• Execute the policy guidelines approved by the Regional Anti-Corruption Commission. • Co-ordinate the preparation and approval of the Regional Government's Anti-Corruption Plans, as well as to monitor compliance. • Reporting on the anti-corruption activities of the Regional Government in public hearings identified by the Regional Anti-Corruption Commission. • Contribute to the observance of the code of ethics and promote investigation, prosecution and punishment of known acts of corruption. • Co-ordinate compliance with the recommendations of control activity. • Organise prevention and citizen empowerment activities. • Propose the short, medium and long-term Institutional Plan for the Fight against Corruption.

Implementing body	Instrument to implement the integrity function	Functions assigned by the implementing instruments
		• Strengthen the Institutional Transparency Portal. • Propose quick intervention procedures for handling complaints on acts of corruption. • Propose educational activities and actions to empower users' and citizens' rights. • Other functions assigned to it.

Source: Information provided by SIP.